wilhelmshöhe park
europe's largest hill park

museumslandschaft
hessen kassel

Published by **Museumslandschaft Hessen Kassel, Bernd Küster**

Project Head **Gisela Bungarten**

Editing **Gisela Bungarten, Sabina Köhler, Lena Weber**

Translation **Susanne Stopfel** (A history of Wilhelmshöhe Park; A tour of Wilhelmshöhe Park), **Christina Oberstebrink** (Timeline)

Graphic design by **augenstern, Büro für Gestaltung, Kassel**

Publishing house **Schnell & Steiner GmbH, Leibnizstraße 13, 93055 Regensburg**

Printed by **Werbedruck GmbH Horst Schreckhase, Spangenberg**

1st edition 2014

ISBN 978-3-7954-2832-7

Bibliographic information published by Deutsche Nationalbibliothek:

The Deutsche Nationalbibliothek lists this publication in the Deutsche Natio-
nalbibliographie; detailed bibliographic data is available on the internet at
http://dnb.ddb.de.

United Nations	Bergpark Wilhelmshöhe
Educational, Scientific and	World Heritage
Cultural Organization	since 2013

The Museumslandschaft Hessen Kassel is an institution of the State of Hesse.

This book was printed with the kind support of
Museumsverein Kassel e. V.

Wilhelmshöhe Park – Europe's largest hill park
Parkbroschüren MHK, vol. 1

Siegfried Hoß

United Nations · **Bergpark Wilhelmshöhe**
Educational, Scientific and · World Heritage
Cultural Organization · since 2013

Contents

A history of Wilhelmshöhe Park 7

Beginnings 8

Grand design: Landgrave Carl 9

Age of transition: Landgrave Friedrich II 14

Romantic and remoulder: Landgrave Wilhelm IX 19

French interregnum 26

The mature landscape park 27

From the court gardeners to the present 30

A tour of Wilhelmshöhe Park 33

1 Lac 37

2 Isle of Roses 37

3 Flora's Vale 39

4 Jussow Waterfall 39

5 Palace 40

6 Ballroom Building 45

7 Service buildings 46

8 Great Greenhouse 47

9 Hall of Socrates and Bowlinggreen 49

10 Fountain Pond 49

11 Jussow Temple 50

12 Aqueduct 51

13 Temple of Mercury 52

14 Vergil's Tomb 54

15 Cestius Pyramid 55

16 The Sibyl's Grotto 56

17 Philosophers' Vale 57

18 Hermitage of Socrates 58

19 Devil's Bridge 59

20 Pluto's Grotto 61

Detour: The Baroque axis 62

21 Steinhöfer Waterfall 68

22 Löwenburg (Lion Castle) 69

23 Löwenburg precincts 71

24 Village of Mulang (Chinese Village) 75

25 Chinese Pagoda 76

26 Cemetery 78

Timeline 81

Glossary 87

Bibliography 90

List of illustrations 93

Picture credits 95

A history of Wilhelmshöhe Park

With a history spanning more than 800 years, the 246-ha Bergpark Wilhelmshöhe is a magnificent example of European garden art. It developed from the original monastery garden, no longer distinguishable today, through the Baroque park laid out from the end of the 17th century, into the 19th-century landscape garden, which in turn was enhanced with neo-Baroque elements in the early years of the 20th century.

During each phase of the park's genesis, earlier stages of artistic design were integrated rather than assimilated into the new layout, ensuring that the manifestations of the 300-year development process are still visible everywhere, and in places preserved in their original fabric.

The Baroque structure on the hilltop came to dominate all the stages succeeding it. The monumental park building provided both a towering landmark for the city and park, and the main theme informing the entire layout: that of the elemental force of water. The genius loci of the dramatic site was harnessed, as it were, to create the spectacular water features set in a unique garden landscape. Next to the stunning feat of engineering represented by the installation of the Hercules statue on top of the Octagon, it was the water features, and the fashioning of the slope into a work of garden art to accommodate them, that were at the core of the nomination for inscription of the Bergpark on the UNESCO World Heritage list. The dramatic presentation of water and the challenges and rewards of laying out a steep slope – those remained the defining factors of all later developments that gradually transformed the property into a landscape park.

This guide is an invitation to you to appreciate and enjoy this extraordinary example of European garden art.

From the foot of the Octagon and the platform above, a vast view opens up – across the park and the city of Kassel to the hills of Kaufunger Wald and the Hoher Meißner range.

Beginnings

Even nine hundred years ago the capabilities and amenities of the site must have been appreciated. The founding of the monastery of Witzenstein, confirmed on 14 December 1143 by the Archbishop of Mainz, stands as proof of the fact. The monastery complex occupied the site now mostly taken up by the Palace's corps de logis; its name, Witzenstein ("White Rock"), was derived from the distinctive light-coloured limestone south-west of today's southern, or Weissenstein, Wing. Secularised in 1527, the former monastery passed into the ownership of the Hessian Landgrave, Philipp the Magnanimous. The further development of the place – and its gardens – was ensured by the demolition of the monastery and the building of a small palace and hunting lodge, embarked upon in 1606 by Landgrave Moritz (r. 1592–1627). The name chosen by Moritz again made reference to the local white stone: he called his little palace "Mauritiolum Leucopetraeum", or "Moritz' place at the White Rock".

Sketch of Weissenstein monastery by Ernst Happel, c. 1550

As well as the usual small garden next to the building itself, a grotto was built in 1615/1616 on the slope west of the palace, the site of today's Pluto's Grotto, and named for its patron. The Moritz Grotto's situation deep inside the forest was quite unusual for its time, but it does show that even then the specific terrain and the element of water were of significance to the laying out of the gardens.

WILHELMSHÖHE von der ALLEE.

The avenue of Königschaussee is the continuation of Wilhelmshöher Allee towards the palace. It was reserved exclusively for the princely family and their visitors. The avenue turns north at the foot of the slope, and approaches the palace by way of another bend. The last stretch is known as Kaleschenweg, or carriage drive.

Grand design: Landgrave Carl

The long reign of Landgrave Carl (r. 1677–1730) was to be of crucial importance both for the city of Kassel and for the park. Carl welcomed French Huguenots persecuted for their faith in their native country to Kassel, which benefited his city economically, causing what was almost a leap forward in its development. At the same time, he was as eager to shine among the European dynasties as any other prince of his time. While other rulers of the Absolutist era tried to garner prestige by building huge palaces, the Hessian Landgrave turned to the laying out of large gardens instead. The Baroque park of Karlsaue was created in the plain, not far from the town palace; another garden was to take shape on the wooded slope rising to the west of Kassel. Here, Carl envisioned something magnificent and never seen before – a water garden taking up the entire hillside. The fact that Carl had a house built for the sole purpose of displaying a small-scale model of the projected layout shows him to have been an exceptional planner.

The house and model are lost; inevitably, speculations on just how far Carl's layout was intended to extend downhill towards the city have remained an intriguing game to the present day.

As early as the 1680s Carl had embarked, more or less simultaneously, on the planning and laying out of his two parks in the plain and on the slope. Actual building had to be preceded by the cutting of swathes through the dense forest to determine the layout's main lines; next came preparatory water-engineering work. From 1696 at the latest, large-scale building was underway on what was to become the Octagon; in 1700 the structure was described as a "mountain of Loniter stone" on the hilltop, already visible from a great distance. From December 1699 to April 1700 Carl was away on a tour of Italy, the "Grand Tour" customarily undertaken by aristocrats and art lovers of the time. He took the opportunity of making an intensive study of Italian gardens and their water features, visiting, among others, the gardens of the Villa d'Este and Villa Aldobrandini. The trip would come

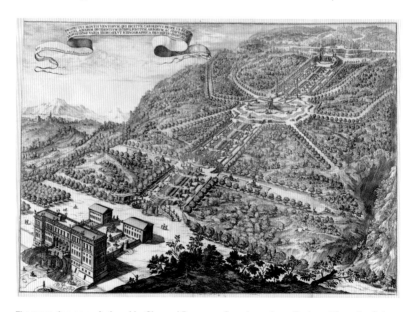

The engraving, commissioned by Giovanni Francesco Guerniero, shows the layout from the Octagon to the planned palace in the 1716 version. In contrast to earlier versions, this one depicts a pyramid and a statue of Hercules on top of the Octagon.

to be of great significance to the further development of the project, as Carl brought back numerous ideas for the embellishment of his water displays.

Carl had succeeded to the title and office in 1677, as a very young man; the usual Grand Tour had to be postponed. In 1699 he was finally in a position to realise his long-cherished desire to visit the cultural sites of Italy. It was probably in Italy that he met the architect Giovanni Francesco Guerniero (c. 1665–1745) and recruited him to the project. Guerniero arrived at Kassel a year later, in the summer of 1701. Initially responsible only for the water engineering and the decoration of the grottoes and Octagon basement, he came to assume responsibility for the entire project over time.

From 1704 onwards Guerniero commissioned a series of engravings (Delineatio Montis) documenting the ambitious undertaking. The best-known of them is the depiction of the distinctive water axis leading from the hilltop to a new palace, built in the style of an Italian villa. Further engravings show numerous details of the planned structure. In this manner, Carl's plans could be made public and propagated well before their completion. The concept and realisation of an artificial water course, seemingly rising within the Octagon and gushing down-hill over a series of cascades, was considered sensational at the time just as it is today.

Building progressed section by section. By 1704, major water-engineering structures and the grotto-style exterior of the Octagon had been completed. In 1708 work on the visually very different upper storey started; from 1713 the pyramid and Hercules statue crowning it were under construction. By 1714 a third of the planned series of cascades was completed; Landgrave Carl commissioned the minting of a medal to commemorate the day it was put into operation. The pictorial and architectural programme was based on Classical mythology.

This view from the collection of engravings commissioned by Giovanni Francesco Guerniero shows the Octagon with its original exterior décor, the Water-Trick Grotto and Artichoke Basin at its foot.

The gods rule on Mount Olympus (characterised by the regular, elegant masonry); below is the world of titans and giants (a rough, grotto-like place), and further down still is the sea or rather, the water with its cascades, Neptune's Basin and Neptune's Grotto.

The Octagon, originally envisioned without the pyramid and Hercules statue but with statues of the Olympian gods gracing its topmost balustrade instead, presented structural problems even during construction. Repairs became necessary early on, and in the course of subsequent modifications the openings of the topmost storey, originally

The engraving by Wolfgang Mayr after a drawing by Johann Georg Fünck ("Prospect of Karlsberg") depicts the complex as realised by Landgrave Carl. In the foreground, a party of courtiers is seen resting beneath an awning and enjoying the view.

On Wednesdays, Sundays and public holidays from 1 May to 3 October the water comes rushing downhill on the stroke of 2.30p.m. as it did in Landgrave Carl's time.

planned as an airy, galleried structure, had to be reduced in size or dispensed with altogether.

In 1717, building came to a temporary conclusion with the installation of the Hercules statue. His work complete, Guerniero had returned to Italy in 1715 to succeed the eminent architect Carlo Fontana in the function as architect in charge of the Acqua Felice, one of Rome's main water conduits.[1]

Landgrave Carl did not live to see his project completed. After his death in 1730, it fell to his heirs to maintain and safeguard the complex. Carl had, however, laid the indelible foundations, creating a basic layout for the Habichtswald hillside that would be of enormous importance later on. The structure he built, and the Hercules statue in particular, remain a striking landmark visible for miles around to the present day.

Age of transition: Landgrave Friedrich II

Carl's sons, Landgrave Friedrich I (r. 1730–1751), who was also King of Sweden, and Landgrave Wilhelm VIII (r. 1751–1760), who acted as his brother's viceregent for many years, governing the destinies of Kassel in troubled times, made no major new contributions to the park. They did, however, keep the structure in good repair as far as possible. With what little money he had available, Wilhelm VIII created a Rococo garden at Wilhelmsthal, about 10 km north of Kassel.

It was Carl's grandson, Landgrave Friedrich II (r. 1760–1785), who continued the work. His reign began during the Seven Years' War, and it was only in 1763, when he returned from exile after the end of the war, that he could take up his duties at Kassel. His work on the park was characteristic of the transitional phase between the Baroque and the landscape garden, something still evident in the plans dating from his time.

1 Cp. Scherner 2012, p. 181–186.

Carl Ferdinand Bosse's magnificent plan of Weissenstein Palace with its gardens and Baroque water features, 1776.

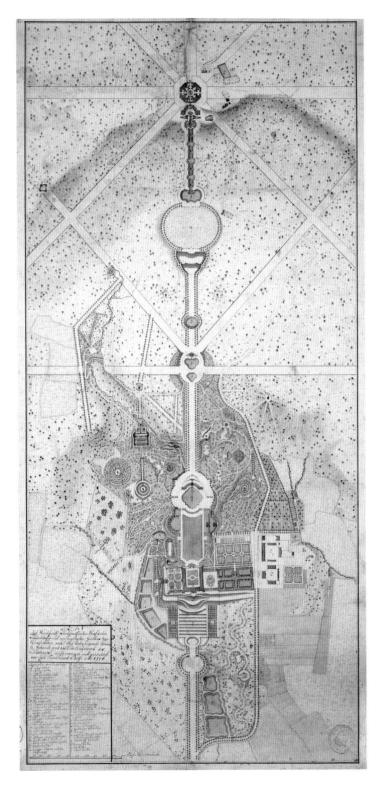

Friedrich II began by opening up the central axis, something that had been planned but not put into practice in Carl's day, laying it out in the Baroque style as an avenue of lime trees. The avenue (today's Wilhelmshöher Allee) continued beyond the palace towards the city, terminating at the gates and what is now Brüder-Grimm-Platz. In the space between the palace and the foot of the Grand Cascade, Friedrich created

The patte d'oie's southern vista terminates at the "Minor Hercules".

a landscape park in an Early Romantic/Sentimental style. From 1770 onwards he was assisted by his court gardener, Daniel August Schwarzkopf (1738–1817), who had received his training in England. It was a park of meandering footpaths and dense vegetation, embellished with numerous shelters, statues and scenic arrangements. The Landgrave also commissioned a number of smaller swathes to create Baroque-style vistas with various park buildings providing points de vue, all of them aligned with the transverse axis in the centre of the park.

View of the Palace after its enlargement by Friedrich II, with the severely shaped Bowlinggreen and the tall fountain. In the valley beyond, the fishponds are just visible.

The intersection of the central and transverse axes was also the point of origin of a patte d'oie (literally, "goose's foot" – three avenues radiating out from one point), its axes leading up to the ridge above. The southernmost axis led to the so-called Minor Hercules built long ago in Landgrave Carl's time.

Water remained a central theme in the park being laid out under Friedrich II too. The fishponds south of the palace, a legacy from the time of the original monastery, were remodelled to a degree, and connected to a stream running down from the so-called Elysium. Friedrich also realised another of Landgrave Carl's dreams: his engineers, namely Philipp Abraham Steinhofer (b. 1739), succeeded in creating the extraordinary fountain envisioned by Carl. The engineer in charge at the time, Denis Papin (1647–1712), had attempted to operate such a fountain by means of a pump. It now rose in the centre of a basin at the back of the so-called Bowlinggreen, operated solely by the water pressure created by the steeply sloping terrain and leaping, according to a contemporary witness,[2] to a height of 43 metres. It was thus one of the tallest in Europe.

At the same time the Renaissance palace built by Landgrave Moritz was considerably altered and enlarged. An orangery was added, and the formal garden layout surrounding the palace with its parterre and hedge garden was main-

• Surviving structures from the Early Romantic/Sentimental phase of the landscape garden: Pluto's Grotto 1766–1768; Vergil's Tomb, c. 1775; Cestius Pyramid, c. 1775; Sibyl's Grotto, c. 1780; Hermitage of Socrates, c. 1775; Mulang village, c. 1782–1785 (however, around 1820 some of the wooden structures were replaced by stone-built versions by the architect Johann Conrad Bromeis, who also made some considerable alterations); Temple of Mercury mentioned (rebuilt in stone by Bromeis c. 1820).
• Surviving trees from the Early Romantic/Sentimental phase of the landscape garden: tulip tree; common oak south-east of the Weissenstein rock.
• Surviving water features: Entenfang Pond; Grand Fountain, pre-1767 (altered in the time of Wilhelm IX).

2 Schmincke 1767, p. 425.

PROSPECT DES FÜRSTLICHEN SCHLOSSES AUF DEM WEISSENSTEIN.
VON DER ABEND SEITE.

View of the Palace; right of centre is the village of Mulang with its Mosque and Pagoda.

tained and extended, which made for a striking contrast with the rest of the garden.

The park was studded with buildings, ornaments and scenic arrangements. There were about fifty of them, and in order to realise them Friedrich II resorted to having some sceneries painted in oils on wooden boards, to complement the small structures, statues and themed plantings. Their sheer number was partly due to Friedrich's ambition to create a park of the Enlightenment by citing and commemorating Classical philosophers. On the other hand, the evoking of an appropriate mood was considered important too: the idea was that visitors should feel emotionally stirred during their walk. For that purpose the most memorable site would have been Pluto's Grotto with its terrifying evocation of an underground domain. The Enlightenment principle of religious tolerance was embodied by a Mosque and a Hermitage of St Paul, neither of which survived; together they were to call the world's religions to mind.

To crown more than twenty years of work on his park, Friedrich II embarked on the building of the Chinese Village (c. 1782–1785). It was a favourite project of the Landgrave's, featuring a Pagoda visible both

from a great distance and from the palace. However, the small ornamental settlement only received its name – and its present appearance – in the time of Friedrich's successor, Wilhelm IX. The name
is probably derived from the term for the Chinese Emperor's hunting
grounds (mulan) rather than the French word for the windmill which
was then part of the complex (moulin). The village was situated next to
a deer park that Wilhelm IX established between it and the Löwenburg,
which also points towards the former explanation for its name.

Several of the small structures were built of wood. From the end of
the 18th century onwards, Wilhelm IX had them gradually replaced by
stone buildings and added several new ones. The original Mosque and
the Banqueting Room were demolished in the 19th century. The village
of Mulang was to be Landgrave Friedrich's last major contribution to
the park.

Romantic and remoulder: Landgrave Wilhelm IX

The work of Friedrich II was cut short by heart failure; it seems, however, as if his son, Landgrave Wilhelm IX (1785–1821, from 1803 Elector Wilhelm I), had seen the new layout of the garden complete before
his eyes when he took up the office. With the young architect Heinrich
Christoph Jussow (1754–1825), who had received part of his training
in England, and the veteran court gardener Daniel August Schwarzkopf the new Landgrave embarked on the third and most compre-
hensive phase in the park's genesis. Fired by the will and creative
determination of Wilhelm IX, the triumvirate transformed the park into
a classical English landscape garden.

In his five-volume standard reference, "Theorie der Gartenkunst"
(1785), the influential garden theoretician and professor of philoso-
phy and art history, Christian Cay Lorenz Hirschfeld (1742–1792), had
praised Landgrave Friedrich II for his imaginative spirit and the wealth
of art in his garden; at the same time he had also found much to criti-
cise, and suggested many improvements. According to Lorenz, there
were fine sceneries; there were, however, too many of them, there

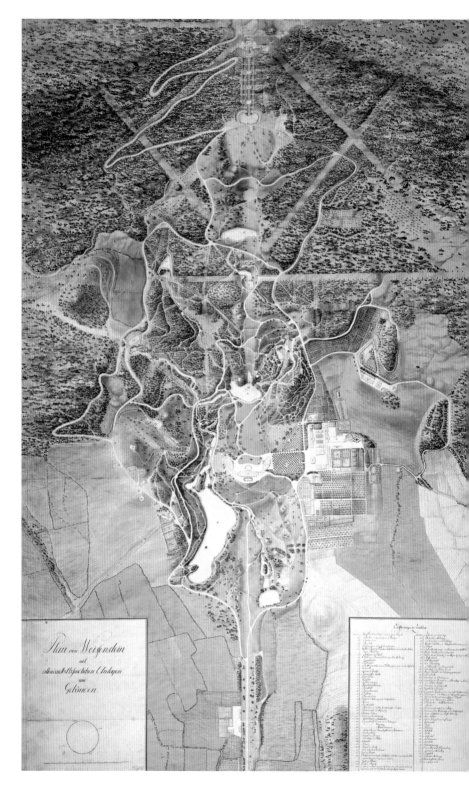

Plan von Weißenstein mit allenneusten bepflanzten Anlagen und Gebäuden

was no overall theme, and some were badly executed and hard to appreciate. The main thrust of his comments was that the number of frequently unconnected follies and ornaments should be reduced, and the park transformed into an integrated whole[3] – an idea adopted and realised within a few years by Wilhelm IX.

He laid down the main structural elements, such as the network of paths and water courses; now the footpaths transversed the park in long s-shaped curves. They appear to be connecting the main structures by sheer serendipity – Wilhelmshöhe Palace (1786–1798), Löwenburg (1793–1801) and Landgrave Carl's Baroque complex as well as the Romantic water features commissioned by Wilhelm himself. The alterations become evident in a plan dated 1796 by Caspar Christoph Schaeffer (1776–1819). Comparison with earlier plans and reports on the progress of the works such as that by Johann Heinrich Müntz (1727–1798) gives an idea of the stunning accomplishment. The decorative excesses were toned down; the Baroque central and transverse axes appear to have been abandoned. However, closer inspection reveals that the Baroque structure has in fact been retained. The dominant central axis survives, both as a visual axis and as the park's calm centre, the foundation block at the core of the design. Even in the transformation by Wilhelm IX, Landgrave Carl's defining layout lives on. A number of follies from the time of Friedrich II and their surroundings were also preserved.

Once again the topography became a design principle. Vistas were created, both within the park and towards the city. The mock-medieval Löwenburg was deliberately set on a knoll so as to be visible from most of the city.

---

3 Hirschfeld 1785, vol. 5, pp. 232–239.

"Plan of Weissenstein" by Caspar Christoph Schaeffer, 1796. It depicts all the buildings and structures in existence at the time as well as the "Wolves' Glen" project, later abandoned.

Johann Heinrich Müntz shows numerous labourers at work, digging the Lac. The soil was used to give a more natural, "landscaped" look to the severely Baroque hillside with the palace.

The dramatic presentation of the elemental force of water as a metaphor of princely power was another aspect Wilhelm IX retained. To increase the amount of water available, he commissioned another supply pipe from the nearby Drusel valley. He also collected the various water courses laid out by his father into one stream transversing the park, and built a number of new water features. Overwhelming in their size and expressive power, they were a worthy match for the Baroque complex with its Cascades and Octagon.

Each of these water features presented the terrifying power of water in its own way: inescapably rushing downhill at the Steinhöfer Waterfall; recalling the famous location in the Alpes the display is named for at Devil's Bridge; as a roaring waterfall and a building seemingly destroyed by an earthquake at the Aqueduct. At the same time, the Aqueduct and the Grand Fountain represent the technological prowess of mankind.

The first of Heinrich Christoph Jussow's structures, the Aqueduct (built 1788–1792), is modelled on a Roman water conduit. The huge and imposing homage to antiquity was unique in Europe at the time – con-

The Steinhöfer Waterfall, with Löwenburg visible in the background. In the bottom right corner, Karl Steinhofer himself is seen greeting some visitors.

temporary garden theory held that large waterfalls must remain the exclusive privilege of Nature.

Another exceptional feature is the Grand Fountain: at the time, fountains were considered unnatural, an outdated Baroque element. Undaunted, Wilhelm IX commissioned the pipe-casting specialist and later inspector of wells, Karl Steinhofer (1747–1829), to make his fountain leap even higher – to about 50 metres. In fact its geyser-like appearance made it uniquely suited to the landscaped surroundings. Here, too, the Landgrave and his architects and gardeners proved themselves to be independent thinkers and creators, quite willing to go directly against contemporary wisdom when deciding what was suitable and appropriate for the park.

Landgrave Wilhelm IX finally came to reap the fruit of the labour generations of his family had expended to establish themselves among the European dynasties: in 1803 he was raised to the rank of Elector, and assumed the title of Elector Wilhelm I. However, only a few years later the advancing armies of Napoleon forced him to flee his electorate and spend the years 1806–1813 in exile. After his return, several more park buildings were added, mostly to enhance existing sceneries; the Jussow Temple overlooking the Fountain Pond is one of them.

At the end of his reign, after almost forty years of work, Wilhelm left behind an exceedingly well-formed park skillfully merging the Baroque structures into an English-style landscape garden. Everything of merit in the earlier layout had been preserved, while the rigid geometry of the basins and hedges from the time of Friedrich II had been broken up. The park as a whole had been transformed according to the principles of the Classical and Romantic landscape garden. However, the tall swathes cut into the forest were maintained; they remained visible well into the 20th century. Large meadows were established, extending even into the fringes of the forest.

The more recent, prominent buildings such as the Palace, Löwenburg and Aqueduct now defined the appearance of the park as much as the Hercules Monument. Their positioning and size created a connection with the Baroque elements. The vistas, the seemingly natural course of the paths and the all-connecting element of water contributed to the homogeneity of the whole. Although every aspect of its design was now informed by the new English style,

• Surviving features from the Romantic phase of the landscape garden: Lac, 1785–1791; Aqueduct, 1788–1792, and Peneus Cascades, from 1786; Bowlinggreen, 1786–1789; Fountain Pond, 1789/1790; Jussow Waterfall, 1791/1792, and Flora's Vale; Isle of Roses, 1793–1795; Devil's Bridge and Hell Pond, 1792/1793; Steinhöfer Waterfall, 1792/1793; Löwenburg, 1793–1801; Felseneck Pavilion, 1794/1795; rebuilt palace: Weissenstein Wing, 1786–1790, Chapel Wing, 1787–1792, corps de logis, 1791–1798; stables, 1791.

• Surviving trees from the Romantic phase of the landscape garden: Numerous individual trees and clusters have survived; however, many are decaying due to their age and will have to be replaced in time. The Weymouth pine next to the Lac is a notable specimen.

Baroque elements such as the central axis had been maintained, their severity tempered by the skillful arrangement of clumps and copses. All of it came together to create the Bergpark Wilhelmshöhe. There is nothing anywhere in the world that compares with the huge water features and infinitely varied water courses. At Kassel they range from the great waterfalls through the cascades, geometric or natural in appearance, the water flowing smoothly or tumbling and foaming, to serene lakes reflecting the morning and evening sun.

In Wilhelm's time the park also gained its current name. The common term for the area adjacent to the Palace, and even the entire park, had hitherto been Weissensteiner Park, the Palace being known as Weissensteiner Schloss. With the completion of his new dwelling in 1798, Wilhelm IX called upon the public to suggest a name for it. The name finally selected, Wilhelmshöhe, was mounted on the side facing

View across the Lac towards the Palace with Löwenburg to the south (left) – one of the park's finest vistas. In the distance is the Octagon with the Hercules statue. Johann Heinrich Bleuler's depiction of 1825 is an impressive portrait of the Bergpark *gesamtkunstwerk*.

the city in large golden letters. It has since come to be used for the Palace, the entire park, and the avenue connecting them with the city. The name of Winterkasten, used in Landgrave Carl's day for the Octagon hilltop, and the term Karlsberg for the slope between the Octagon and the Palace, are still used to describe these specific areas. Elector Wilhelm I died in 1821. In accordance with his will he was laid to rest in the Löwenburg crypt.

French Interregnum

Napoleon's campaign through most of Europe did not spare the electorate of Hesse. Elector Wilhelm I fled Kassel in 1806; in 1807 the Treaties of Tilsit created the new kingdom of Westphalia, with Kassel as its capital and Napoleon's youngest brother Jérôme Bonaparte (r. 1807–1813, as Jérôme Napoleon) as its king. Jérôme, too, appreciated the setting: in November 1806 he took up residence in the Palace with his spouse, Princess Katharina of Württemberg. During his time, Wilhelmshöhe was renamed Napoleonshöhe. The park was not interfered with, but neither was it properly maintained. The statues of Pluto's Grotto, depicting the gods of the netherworld, were lost in those years. However, today's Ballroom Building was first commissioned by Jérôme Bonaparte.

Originally a theatre (plays were shown twice a week), it was built in 1808–1810 by Leo von Klenze (1784–1864), and in 1828–1830 it was converted into a ballroom by Johann Conrad Bromeis (1788–1855). A paned gallery building, somewhat Chinese in appearance and lavishly furnished with aviaries, fountains and flower arrangements, provided Jérôme with sheltered access from the Chapel Wing to the theatre. On special occasions it was brilliantly illuminated. After the return of Wilhelm I the structure was relocated to the Mulang, where it probably graced the pheasant house until well into the 1830s.

Torrents of water tumbling down the New Waterfall

The mature landscape park

The Electors succeeding Wilhelm I – Wilhelm II (r. 1821–1831) and Friedrich Wilhelm (r. 1831–1866) polished and refined the park without making any more large-scale alterations to its core parts. Wilhelm II extended the landscape garden to include the area north of the original park, where Wilhelm I had already purchased a small farm which was used as a dairy. Under Wilhelm II, the influence of the landscape gardeners in charge grew considerably. Court Gardener Wilhelm Hentze (1822–1864) in particular played a decisive role in the shaping of the park. As well as the garden at Wilhelmshöhe, Hentze also developed those of Wilhelmsthal and Karlsaue, and the Gesundbrunnenpark at Hofgeismar.

His work was characterised by a talent for creating seemingly natural settings. Shrubs and trees were combined into clumps; open spaces were enlivened by the play of light and shade. Solitary trees, groves and harmonious groups composed of various types of tree were planted, and could be appreciated from skillfully laid out paths. To achieve this natural appearance, Hentze did not limit himself to native trees – exotic species with coloured foliage were used as well. The

The rocky walls of the New Waterfall still convey an idea of the magnificent water display of yore.

sloping terrain allowed the creation of vistas towards the city. In this mature version of the landscape park, follies are a minor element, sometimes dispensed with altogether. The focus is on the idealisation of Nature instead, which is achieved by the thoughtful arrangement of water, trees, lawns and paths. It was nevertheless a building that served as the prelude, as it were, to the park – if one perceived as a natural phenomenon rather than a man-made structure. This was the New Waterfall, constructed by the inspector of wells, Karl Steinhofer, in 1822–1828. It is still considered

The oak grove enchants with its ever-changing play of light.

Steinhofer's masterpiece, not so much as a feat of engineering but as a magnificent work of art. Standing on the bridge at the foot of the waterfall, spectators must have felt that the water, cascading towards them over three separate falls each 16 m wide, was going to sweep them away. A reservoir further uphill provided sufficient water; however, an inadequate substructure in the sandy soil soon necessitated repairs (in 1835 and in the 1850s), and in 1943 the water feature was shut down permanently. The towering walls of stone still convey something of the awe the waterfall must have inspired.

The decommissioning of the New Waterfall is regrettable as its wide, tall falls make for an overwhelming image of the primeval force of water, and Steinhofer's last creation is also the conclusion of the park's scenic water features.

• Surviving structures from the phase of the mature landscape park: New Waterfall, 1822–1828; Great Greenhouse, 1822; stables, altered and in part relocated 1822; Guardhouse, 1824–1826; cavalier house (now an administrative building), 1825, relocated to a site further north.

• Surviving park features from the phase of the mature landscape park: the garden landscape at New Waterfall, 1822–1835.

• Surviving notable trees from the phase of the mature landscape park: pedunculate oak next to the Fountain Pond; North American oaks; tulip trees on Tulpenallee.

The park expansion of 1822–1835 is the only one that has not been transformed by a later gardening style. It presents the "realistic", mature landscape garden in its purest form.

In 1822/1823, the Great Greenhouse was built for the displaying of non-hardy plants. With the flower clumps planted in front of it, it provides a backdrop on the northern side of the Pleasureground, screening the service buildings from

The Great Greenhouse as depicted in its original appearance (c. 1826) on a teapot. The china set included numerous pieces decorated with sights from the Wilhelmshöhe Park.

view. The central pavilion, originally circular in layout, was replaced with the imposing rectangular structure seen today in the course of a thorough restoration (1884–1888). With its glassed south front, stone walls and covered roofs on the north side of the wings, the building occupies an architectural middle ground between the tradition of the orangery and that of the modern greenhouse. The use of iron elements as well as traditional wooden ones, and the steel and glass structure of the central pavilion of 1888, make it one of the earliest iron and glass buildings in existence.

From the court gardeners to the present

European politics determined the fate of the ruling princes of Kassel once again when Prussia defeated the German Confederation in 1866. The electorate of Hesse was annexed, and Kassel became the capital of the Prussian province of Hesse-Nassau. The end of the electorate, however, did not spell the end of garden art at Wilhelmshöhe. The German Emperor declared the Wilhelmshöhe a crown estate and reserved its use for the imperial family to spend their summers there. The electorate's garden administration was replaced with a local department of the imperial garden administration at Potsdam-Sanssouci.

Because of the regular visits by the imperial family, the park was cared for and developed further; towards the end of the century the area surrounding the palace was embellished with the then fashionable carpet beds. The first court gardener of the Prussian administration, Franz Vetter (active 1864–1891), restored overgrown swathes and created new vistas. Areas of densely growing conifers were replaced with airier arrangements of deciduous trees and shrubs, especially on Apollo Hill and next to the Lac.

Another notable name is that of the court gardener, and later garden director, Ernst Virchow (active 1899–1918). In 1903 he submitted the first plan of Wilhelmshöhe drawn up after the time of Wilhelm I. It depicts a mature, fully formed landscape park, the respective heights

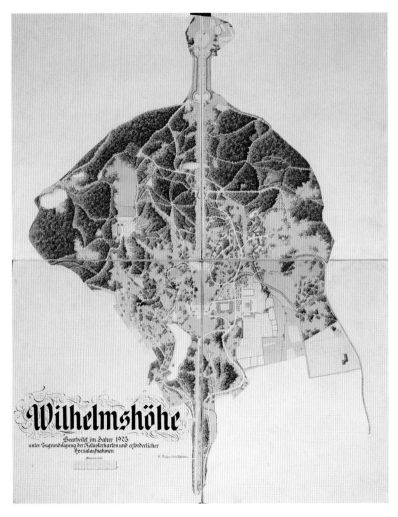

Ernst Virchow summarises 200 years of the park's history in this plan of 1903 – a unique European gesamtkunstwerk depicted in a strikingly original and decorative manner.

of the various wooded areas shown in different shades of green, showing a well-balanced composition of densely planted spaces and open meadows or bodies of water. The park has grown into a unified, harmonious whole, a gesamtkunstwerk for visitors to explore on a network of paths.

The plan also demonstrates the design principles applied in the arrangement of the groves and solitary trees to achieve a particular spatial effect. Frequently solitaire trees are placed in front of densely wooded areas, breaking up the fringes. Deep bays in the edges of the forest allow the meadows to spread between the trees. By contrast, the centre of the park is characterised by a lively interplay of open spaces and small copses. The plan also shows that the park's homogeneity benefited from its extension towards the north, illustrating two hundred years of history in Virchow's highly individual design language. Since the drawing up of Virchow's plan, only a few structures have been added to the park, namely the Orchard House (post-1900) and the new Hercules Visitor Centre (2009–2011). The Schlosshotel, destroyed during WWII, has since been rebuilt in the architectural style of the 1950s.

A tour of Wilhelmshöhe Park

The following tour of the park covers the major features, and may start at any given point. Then again, it is just as well to set out with no instruction whatsoever, guided only by the paths that show the way through the park, referring to the guidebook only when additional information on the individual features is wanted or required. As our overview of the park's history has shown, in places there are layers of its development overlying each other, as it were; a walk in the park is thus a walk through its long and varied history.

For your guidance, here is a short overview of the successive design phases that shaped the park:
- Renaissance garden: Landgrave Moritz the Scholar (1606–1627)
- Baroque garden: Landgrave Carl (1680s–1730)
- Early Romantic/Sentimental English or landscape park:
  Landgrave Friedrich II (1760–1785)
- Romantic landscape park: Landgrave Wilhelm IX (1785–1802),
  later Elector Wilhelm I (1803–1821)
- Mature landscape park: Elector Wilhelm II (1821–1831) and
  Elector Friedrich Wilhelm (1831–1866)
- Further development of the landscape park and neo-Baroque
  phase, for the most part supervised by Court Gardeners Vetter
  and Virchow (1866–1918)

The tour focuses chiefly on the Early Romantic/Sentimental (1760–1785) and Romantic (1785–1821) phases of the garden's history. The era of the Baroque garden (1696–1730) will be discussed in the form of a detour, while that of the mature landscape park (1821–1866) has been described in the history of the garden (p. 27ff). The tour as described here will take approximately 3.5 hours. It will start at the Lac, taking you through Flora's Vale with the Isle of Roses, past the Palace and uphill towards the Aqueduct. From there it will lead you to Vergil's Tomb, the Pyramid and the Sibyl's Grotto.

The Lac, with the Palace beyond

Through the Philosophers' Vale and past the Entenfang Pond you will reach Socrates' Hermitage and then Pluto's Grotto and the Devil's Bridge. This is where you can make a detour to see the Baroque water features. A wide arc will take you to Löwenburg via the Steinhöfer Waterfall, and past the deer park and the village of Mulang back to your starting point. Before we describe the highlights of the tour in sequence, a topographic peculiarity of the park should be pointed out. The Bergpark covers approximately 246 ha on the eastern slope of the Habichtswald hill. As well as sheer size, there is the fairly rugged terrain to consider which has inspired architects and landscape gardeners through the centuries to come up with brilliant responses. The difference in altitude between the Octagon and the Palace is more than 240 m, and the terrain drops by another 75 m towards the eastern end of the park. The incomparable water features were built to exploit this drop.

Previous pages: Wolves' Glen looking towards the Palace

① Lac

Immediately after his accession to the title, in 1785, Wilhelm IX
embarked on the conversion of the fish ponds dating back to the times
of the monastery into a seemingly natural lake, which was extended
considerably towards the south. The work took until 1791; large quan-
tities of soil had to be excavated, and deposited again on the side facing the valley. Only cohesive, that is to say clayey, soil could be used;
everything else had to be discarded. Moreover, the soil contained
numerous blocks of quartzite that had to be broken up with explosives
before they could be moved. A large calm lake reflecting the early sun-
light took shape, giving that area the character of a morning garden.
The cascades marking the lake's inlet and outlet were designed by
Heinrich Christoph Jussow (1791/1792, 1798). A walk by the shore
offers numerous fine views towards the Palace, the village of Mulang
and the Hercules Monument.

② Isle of Roses

As early as c.1767, Friedrich II had commissioned Daniel August
Schwarzkopf to create a "cabinet of roses". The Isle of Roses, laid
out in tandem with the construction of the new Palace (1786–1798)
and the Lac, provided a new setting for the Landgrave's collection
of roses. It was constructed between 1789 and 1795 using materials
from the demolished palace of Weissenstein.

Schwarzkopf was not merely in charge of the garden layout, he was
a successful rose-grower himself. One variety introduced by him, the
"Pearl of Weissenstein", is still available and on display in the park.
Paintings by Johann Heinrich Tischbein the Elder show roses to have
been planted not just on the island itself but all around it as well,
in the shape of deliberately irregular groups of shrubs. The collection attracted attention well beyond the borders of Hesse; it is hardly
surprising that in 1808 the Landgrave should have commissioned his
court miniaturist, Salomon Pinhas (1759–1837), to immortalise it in a
series of 133 watercolours. The paintings were originally intended for

The "Pearl of Weissenstein" grown by Schwarzkopf, drawn from nature by Salomon Pinhas, 1806.

publication; however, they never appeared in print. By the time Wilhelmshöhe passed into Prussian ownership (1866) if not earlier, the collection of roses had fallen into oblivion. It was only rediscovered in the 1970s, and it is thanks to a private initiative of rose lovers that the Isle of Roses and its surroundings have been re-stocked with numerous shrub and climbing roses. Pinhas' rose portraits were finally pub-

The painting by Johann Heinrich Tischbein the Elder shows roses growing at the foot of the "White Rock", well outside the Isle of Roses.

lished in 2001, in a magnificent volume of facsimiles.

3 Flora's Vale

The vale between the stream running from Fountain Pond to the Isle of Roses and the Bowlinggreen has been named for the statue of Flora it shelters, assigning the Roman goddess of flowers and natural growth a place in the immediate vicinity of the Palace.

Statue of Flora by the Heyd brothers

In the days of Friedrich II, the river Styx was meandering its way through the Elysian Fields, the land of the Blessed, in this small valley. At that time it also held statues of various Classical deities including one of Venus. From 1792 onwards, the vale was enlarged and transformed into a flower garden graced by the sandstone statue of Flora, a replica of the Flora Farnesina sculpted by the brothers Ludwig Daniel and Johann Wolfgang Heyd.

In the years after WWII, a tradition of concerts established itself in the park. Originally the venue was the Ballroom Building, but in the 1950s a pavilion in the architectural style of the time was built in Flora's Vale to provide a weather-resistant shelter for the musicians.

4 Jussow Waterfall

In the time of Wilhelm IX the park's water courses were redesigned almost from scratch. The various ditches and streams from the days of Friedrich II were joined to form one major stream, with the large water displays arranged along its course.

The stream connecting the Fountain Pond to the Lac was reshaped as well, and in 1791/1792 the architect, Jussow, made good use of

The amount of water splashing down between the rocks of the Jussow Waterfall is considerably larger when the displays are in operation. Hidden beyond the waterfall's edge is the Island of the Blessed.

the difference in altitude by constructing a new waterfall south of the Palace. For that purpose he divided the stream coming down from the Fountain Pond into two arms to create an island, and at its lower end a natural-looking waterfall of large quartzite rocks. Here, too, Elysian imagery is invoked: according to the myth the land is surrounded by Okeanos, and only the chosen may set foot on it. Even today there are no boats available; the island with its tall thuja trees is reached by way of stepping stones embedded in the stream.

⑤ Palace

The heart of the park has always been at this very spot. In the Middle Ages the site was occupied by the monastery of Witzenstein with its gardens, meadows and fishponds. Later, Landgrave Moritz had his Renaissance palace, "Moritzheim am Weissenstein", built here. Today's three-wing structure was planned and built in three stages. The southern or Weissenstein Wing was constructed in 1786 as a palace in itself (Weissensteinschloss) from plans by Wilhelm's architect Simon Louis du Ry (1726–1799). He was the last of a family of eminent Huguenot architects, the Du Rys, three generations of whom had been working for the Landgraves since Carl's time. The palace of Moritzheim, situated on the central axis, remained in use. The second building phase comprised the construction of the Chapel Wing (from 1788) with its three-aisled chapel north of the central axis. A number of proposals were submitted for the new corps de logis (1791–1798), which was to replace the old palace. Sitting on the park's main axis, it was considered to be detrimental to the main vista of the landscape park; in some proposals it was consequently replaced with an obelisk or a memorial to the great inspirer, Landgrave Carl. However, in the end it was the design by Heinrich Christoph Jussow that prevailed, the veteran architect who had already created many of the park's buildings and sceneries.

With the addition of two storeys to the galleries originally connecting the wings, the palace acquired its present-day appearance in 1829.

The Palace, its wings still largely unconnected. They were later joined together into a single structure.

In the evenings, even with the illuminated water features for competition, the Palace still shines.

The central part was originally surmounted by a dome, but this was destroyed in WWII and not rebuilt afterwards. After the war, in 1968–1974, major repairs took place, and Wilhelmshöhe Palace was converted into a museum. In 2000, the State of Hesse commissioned another major renovation and refurbishment. Today, the ground floor houses the Collection of Antiquities, while the Old Masters are on display on the upper floors. A small bistro (Café Jérôme) and the museum shop are located in the basement.

The connection between the palace and park is best experienced on the first floor. In the Florasaal room eight "ideal prospects" of the park as envisioned by the Landgrave are on display. Painted from 1716 over the span of thirteen years, five of them by the hand of Jan van Nickelen (1656–1721), the others by his son Rymer (active c. 1721–c. 1740), they depict Landgrave Carl's vision of a water garden encompassing the entire hillside, the later ones focusing on the lower part of the water axis and the palace. From the western windows the view is towards the Hercules Monument along the central axis; in the east it is along Wilhelmshöher Allee towards Kassel.

In the lobby of the Weissenstein Wing, which still contains rooms furnished with pieces from the time of the Landgraves and Electors, the large original plan by Caspar Christoph Schaeffer dated 1796 is on display; it depicts the transformative phase during the reign of Wilhelm IX in impressive detail.

The three-wing Palace complex is the point de vue of many of the park's vistas – here it is seen from Pluto's Grotto.

In the northern or Chapel Wing, the original chapel has been preserved; it is still used for services and weddings. The wing also houses the Print Room and a large reference library of approximately 125,000 volumes, as well as the headquarters of Museumslandschaft Hessen Kassel.

Although its function may have changed, the Palace is still the dominant centrepiece of the park, with numerous vistas radiating out from it.

For those in a hurry, the flight of stairs in the palace courtyard looking out towards the Hercules offers an ideal position from which to appreciate the Bergpark and gain an overview of its history. A fan of three vistas opens up as if to display every phase of the park's genesis. The central axis is dominated by Landgrave Carl's forty-metre-high Octagon on the hilltop, surmounted by the Pyramid (26 m), base (3 m) and

The place to be for those in a hurry, with vistas radiating out towards sights from every phase of the park. On the left is Löwenburg; in the centre and halfway up the hill is Pluto's Grotto and above it, the Octagon and Hercules; to the right of the central axis are the Jussow Temple and Bowlinggreen with the (partially hidden) Hall of Socrates; on the right the third axis leads towards Apollo Hill.

copper statue of Hercules (8 m). At the foot of the Octagon are the Baroque Cascades, impressive even at those times when no water is running down them. Halfway down the axis is Pluto's Grotto from the era of Friedrich II, which replaced the Renaissance-era Moritz Grotto. Beyond the Bowlinggreen is the Fountain Pond, with the Jussow Temple (commissioned by Elector Wilhelm I after his return from exile) somewhat off-centre. Immediately in front of the palace is a carpet bed dating from the time of the German Emperors.

A slight turn towards the left brings Löwenburg into view, built for Landgrave Wilhelm IX in the early days of his reign. One of the park's peculiarities becomes evident here: there is no long visual axis leading up to it; it is the positioning of the main structures relative to each other, and the skillful use of the terrain, that creates the vistas. Another turn, towards the right this time, brings another carpet bed into view. Beyond it is a landscaped area framed by copses, with no apparent point de vue. Here Friedrich II had positioned his Temple of Apollo with its view towards the city. The temple was demolished in 1817; the small piece of scenery now serves as a prelude, as it were, to the mature landscape park with its idealised nature and the New Waterfall. This part of the park is accessed by the path at the foot of the so-called Apollo Hill, and by another footpath snaking up the small hill.

⑥ Ballroom Building

In the days of Friedrich II a small formal garden with a Four Seasons Pavilion had occupied the site where King Jérôme built a court theatre in 1808–1810.

The chestnut trees planted under Wilhelm IX were spared, and the theatre was set inside the "quincunx" (i.e. the arrangement of five eyes on the side of a die) formed by the trees. The structure, converted into a ballroom by Johann Conrad Bromeis in 1828, was the first major building by Leo von Klenze, who would go on to build the Munich Pinakothek. In the course of Bromeis' conversion of the neo-Classical building it received its magnificently painted interior décor of flower arrangements and birds. Today it is used for musical events and readings. In the post-war years the chestnut trees surrounding the building were lost, but in 2001/2002 the setting was restored on the basis of historical documents.

The interior of the Ballroom Building with its magnificently painted walls and ceilings.

❼ Service buildings

The stables were built 1791 in the early neo-Classical style, a three-wing structure surrounding a courtyard, and enlarged in 1822. On its north-western side the so-called Gardener's House is built on to it, connected to the stables proper by a single-storey building.

At the northern end of the courtyard is the Riding Hall with its magnificent self-supporting roof construction spanning the 30 x 18 m interior. Today the hall is used for events. The service area also includes the carriage house (today part of the hotel and housing its conference rooms), the Ökonomie (originally housing the kitchens and bakery, today a residential building) and the Schlosshotel, rebuilt after the original hotel was destroyed in WWII. To the west and in line with the stables are the cavalier house, today an administrative building, and behind it the nursery. East are the café in the former Old Guardhouse, and the Old Post Office, now housing Wilhelmshöhe's museum education services.

A bird's eye view of the service area with the nursery (A), stables (B), Gardener's House (C), Riding Hall (D), Ökonomie (E), Carriage House (F), Schlosshotel (G), Old Guardhouse (H) and the cavalier house (I); at the far right are the Great Greenhouse (J) and Ballroom Building (K).

8 Great Greenhouse

The Great Greenhouse, built by Johann Conrad Bromeis from 1822, served three functions. For one, it provided a background north of the Pleasureground, the ornamental area adjacent to the Palace, creating an enclosed space containing the Bowlinggreen and the area in front of the Planthouse, as the Great Greenhouse was called at the time.

For another, it housed numerous exotic plants, among them the pisang, otherwise known as the banana tree, which had grown too large for the other greenhouses. The circular central pavilion (or "Salon") was also used for prestigious functions and for receiving visitors. The striking central structure we see today is one of the earliest examples of the steel and glass buildings developed in the 19th century. However, even the dome preceding it had already been a cast-iron and glass construction. After numerous repairs, a thorough overhaul in 1884–1887 saw the dome replaced with today's rectangular structure. The tradition of using the so-called coldhouse plants to decorate the space in front of the greenhouse during the summer is still carried on today.

Looking up may have its rewards too: Exotic palm trees seen against the elaborate steel and glass roof construction of the central pavilion.

Carpet beds in front of the Great Greenhouse. The arrangement seen in the bottom left corner is composed of coldhouse plants, planted out in their pots in summer.

In winter, the east wing houses the camellias, the western one, a variety of plants from South America, Australia and the Mediterranean. In the central pavilion, tropical plants such as banana trees, palms and orchids are cultivated all year round, with many of them planted out in summer.

Towards the end of the 19th century, elaborate carpet beds were laid out south of the Great Greenhouse and next to the Palace; between 2003 and 2005 they were restored on the basis of research and historical models. The Wilhelmshöhe gardener, Paul Böhne, co-authored the standard reference on the subject of carpet bedding, which consequently contains patterns taken from the Wilhelmshöhe garden including the names of the plants used. Even today the planting pattern, changed annually, is taken from the book "Album für Teppichgärtnerei", first published in the 19th century.[4]

4 Goetze, no year [1900].

⑨ Hall of Socrates and Bowlinggreen

The Bowlinggreen is the calm and level area in front of the Palace, providing both an empty space for the Palace to appear to its best advantage, and – when considered from the Palace itself – an opening into the park's spaces, directing the spectator's eye towards the various sceneries. The lack of a central path challenges the visitor to choose one of the two leading away on either side, and follow where it leads.

The Hall of Socrates, a semicircular, columned hall, was built by Heinrich Christoph Jussow in 1813–1816 on the edge of the Bowlinggreen. The structure is also known as the Semicircular Temple, or simply the Bowlinggreen Temple. It is characterised by its six Ionic columns supporting the entablature. The back wall was originally pierced, and urns graced the roof. The small building has no function other than to embellish the park and create a point de vue.

⑩ Fountain Pond

The Fountain Pond on the park's central axis marks the boundary between the level area surrounding the Palace and Bowlinggreen, and the slope rising towards the Octagon.

On Wednesdays, Sundays and public holidays from 1 May to 31 October, the water features come to a dazzling climax with the 50-m fountain rising from its pond. Originally a formal basin with the fountainhead in the centre, the pond acquired its natural appearance (and the fountain its full height) only in the Romantic era. However, even thirty years earlier the inspector of wells, Philipp Abraham Steinhofer, had constructed the tallest fountain ever seen, 43 metres high and operated solely by exploiting the natural drop between Hell Pond and the fountain basin. The further increase in height was achieved by Steinhofer's brother Karl, his junior by eight years, who fed the fountain from a basin situated higher even than Hell Pond.

The 50-m fountain operates on water pressure created by the 80-m drop between the reservoir and the Fountain Pond. The crowning glory of the park's water features, it rises in the shape of a natural geyser.

⑪ Jussow Temple

Heinrich Christoph Jussow's temple with its open ambulatory, built 1817–1818, was modelled on the Temple of Ancient Virtue in the land-scape park of Stowe, England. At Kassel, however, it was named for its creator rather than dedicated to a Classical deity, suggesting that the beauty and further embellishment of the park took priority over metaphysics in this case.

Fine detail in the capitals of the Jussow Temple

⑫ Aqueduct

The Aqueduct was built 1788–1792 under the direction of Heinrich Christoph Jussow, in the shape of a ruin built of tuff stone. Jussow recreated a Roman water conduit supported by 14 tall arches. At its highest point, emphasised by a ruinous watchtower, the conduit branches off in two directions. One branch ends inconspicuously and almost immediately; the other one is only a few metres long. However, the structure is not merely a bland folly. Like the Classical aqueduct it is modelled on, it is capable of conducting water – which then tumbles down from the broken end with elemental force, a 30-m waterfall. More water rushes down into the gorge below over stones arranged so as to suggest buildings destroyed in an earthquake. In this manner, yet another terrifying force of nature is portrayed.

The image of the ruinous Roman aqueduct reflects the era's fascination with Classical antiquity and its architectural and cultural heritage. Moreover, in this manner Wilhelm IX could realise yet another spectacular waterfall presented as part of a natural landscape. The Aqueduct is one of the park's most important structures, especially among the water displays (see also Parkbroschüre MHK, vol. 2, water features).

From the Aqueduct waterfall, the water runs down the Peneus Cascades towards the Fountain Pond.

Almost a century earlier, Landgrave Carl had created the Octagon and the Cascades at its foot, evoking an image of water seemingly rising within a wellhouse and tumbling down from it. Here the metaphor is repeated in the contemporary visual language of the landscape park: now it is the Aqueduct that provides the wellhouse. The Peneus Cascades a little further downstream conduct the water towards the Fountain Pond. North of the Aqueduct, visitors have another opportunity to take a detour towards the New Waterfall and the mature landscape park.

⑬ Temple of Mercury

From the Aqueduct, a view opens towards the Temple of Mercury on the slope above. It was built around 1780, in the time of Friedrich II, as an open circular temple. The park building was modelled on the Temple of Venus in the English landscape garden of Stowe.

Both the dome, which had been destroyed in WWII, and the lost leaden statue of Mercury have been reinstalled in 2010–2012, in the course of the restoration of park buildings. The dome has been executed as a wooden construction tiled with slate, as depicted in historical photographs. The statue of Mercury, by the sculptor Hermann Leber, is a modern interpretation decided on after a design competition: a reconstruction of the original statue proved to be impossible due to insufficient source material.

Analysis has revealed the original colour scheme of light-coloured columns and cornices and an ultramarine-based blue for the interior of the dome, which has now been restored.
The footpath branching off towards the Temple of Mercury from the main path offers a small spectacle. It runs along the bank of a seemingly natural stream – the one that used to feed the New Waterfall.

Before the Temple of Mercury appears on a small elevation at the end of a meadow, it is already visible as a reflection on the surface of the

The replica of a Roman water conduit was created with much elaborate detail. The ruinous-look-ing masonry on the right suggests both the collapsed part of the Aqueduct and additional build-ings, all seemingly destroyed by an earthquake.

The Temple of Mercury after the re-erection of its dome and a general overhaul, with the new statue of Mercury designed by Hermann Leber.

stream. The playful use of mirror effects, surprises and illusions is another design principle from all three phases of the landscape garden.

⑭ Vergil's Tomb

Our tour turns left beneath one of the Aqueduct's arches and takes us to Vergil's Tomb, built around 1775. This park folly from the Early Romantic/Sentimental phase of the landscape garden is dedicated to the great poet, and the shape given to it – that of a burial place –

Vergil's Tomb is a replica of what is believed to be the great poet's actual burial place in Naples.

makes it a place of sentimental remembrance at the same time. Its architectural model is the Tomb of Vergil near Naples, even though it is unknown whether Vergil (70–19 BC) was indeed buried on Mount Posillipo. More than anything else it was Vergil's pastoral poetry, also known as Bucolica, that informed our culture's notion of Arcadia. Even today bucolic is a term describing a serene, unspoiled setting comparable to the ideal of Arcadia. In the small grassy dell spreading out in front of the tomb, the image has been converted into a romantic park scenery.

⑮ Cestius Pyramid

The Cestius Pyramid belongs to the same era as Vergil's Tomb. A closer look at the plan of the park dating from the time of Friedrich II shows that the two sepulchral monuments are positioned symmetrically on both sides of the central axis: they are clearly meant to refer

The Cestius Pyramid recalls the burial monument of the Roman praetor, Caius Cestius.

to each other. The building is believed to be modelled on the monumental tomb of Caius Cestius at Rome, although the Kassel pyramid
has been known by several names:

It was called the Egyptian Pyramid at first, and later Homer's Tomb;
today it is universally known as the Cestius Pyramid. Both funereal
follies are among the few remaining examples of the innumerable park
buildings, statues, and garden rooms created, in the early years of the
park's Early Romantic/Sentimental phase, in the deliberately "wild"
stretches north and south of the main axis. The path leading to the
Hermitage of Socrates and the footpath meandering up the slope still
follow the course set for them in the days of Friedrich II. At one time,
only the stumps remained of the larches that had once been shading
the path. By reference to historical plans and after making sure of
their original positions, they could be replanted. Today the path is once
more, like many footpaths from those years, lined by larches.

⑯ The Sibyl's Grotto

The Sibyl's Grotto, built 1769–1772, is yet another feature dating from
the Early Romantic/Sentimental phase of the park's history. According to contemporary documents, the room at the end of the vaulted
passage, 5 x 5.5 m in size and 5 m in height, once housed a statue
of the Sibyl. The ceiling had caved in by 1863, but the room is due for
restoration in the next few years. The model for the Sibyl's Grotto is
said to have been the grotto of the Cumaean Sibyl near Naples.

The Sibyls were the oracular seeresses of Classical antiquity, mortal
but long-lived; in the throes of prophetic ecstasy, they foretold the –
usually calamitous – future. The Cumaean Sibyl is among the most
prominent of her kind, with numerous myths to her name. By a ruse
she managed to live to the very respectable age of a thousand years
but, having neglected to ask for perpetual youth as well, her ageing
body shrank until she lived in a pottery jar suspended from the ceiling. It was she who foretold the fate of Rome; her predictions were
recorded in books and consulted when important decisions were at

Entrance doorway of the Sibyl's Grotto

hand. The Cumaean Sibyl also told Aeneas, founder of Rome, the way to Elysium, where he was bound in search of his father (according to Vergil's founding legend of Rome).

The Wilhelmshöhe Park's own Elysium (today's Jussow Waterfall) is situated not far from the Sibyl's Grotto, making for a fine connection, intellectually as well as spatially.

⑰ Philosophers' Vale

From the Sibyl's Grotto, a path leads uphill and through the so-called Philosophers' Vale, a term not found on any map of the park. However, Hirschfeld described the little shelters built here in the time of Friedrich II, summarised them under the term Philosophers' Vale, and then developed the concept further.[5] The name has survived, even though the philosophers' huts (there were dwellings for Archimedes, Anax-

5 Hirschfeld 1785, vol. 5, p. 235 f.

agoras and Democritus, among others) in the small grassy dell have not. Landgrave Friedrich's notion that a park should be considered an educational institution becomes evident here, a notion clearly shared by Hirschfeld: "The Philosophers' Vale in particular I would preserve and enhance. [...] Opening a door, one might perceive this or that Greek sage, represented naturally and fully life-sized in characteristic garb, occupied with something that is appropriate for him to do [...]. This vale of philosophers should become one of the most interesting sceneries."[6] He also proposed displaying the respective philosophers' writings in each hut for the perusal of visitors.

⑱ Hermitage of Socrates

The Enlightenment ideals that informed the Philosophers' Vale are also at work in the Hermitage of Socrates further uphill. The original wooden structure was rebuilt early in the 19th century, as a stone building with a portico supported by two columns. The front is faced with bark, while the gable, door and doorframe are painted with elaborate bark patterns representing different types of tree.

The Hermitage of Socrates after restoration, 2012

6 Hirschfeld 1785, vol. 5, p. 235 f.

The interior featured decorative figures – Hirschfeld describes the topic as "Socrates reading in prison".[7] The scene may have been cast in plaster, or even just painted on to the wall. A statue of Socrates created in 1782 by the sculptor brothers Ludwig Daniel and Johann Wolfgang Heyd has not survived, and neither has a wooden trellis with climbing plants that covered the exterior wall early in the 20th century. One notable feature is the long view across Kassel: ever since the Hermitage was built, the spruce-lined swathe has been guiding the view down towards the Lac and beyond it, over the city of Kassel and on towards the hills of Kaufunger Wald just visible on the horizon.

⑲ Devil's Bridge

Situated south of Pluto's Grotto, the Devil's Bridge scenery with Heinrich Christoph Jussow's spectacular waterfall is yet another major attraction. Originally the setting was even more dramatic as it was a wooden bridge spanning the chasm. In contrast to the Aqueduct, the Devil's Bridge setting is taken directly from nature. On the one hand, it expresses a fervent admiration for the scenic beauties of the Alps. On the other, it provides yet another opportunity for a dramatic display of huge volumes of water.

The bridge spans the 10-m waterfall in a slight curve. The neo-Gothic cast-iron construction by Johann Conrad Bromeis was installed in 1826 to replace the earlier, wooden structure.

Plans from the time of Wilhelm IX refer to the small natural pond beneath Devil's Bridge as "reservoir for the Aqueduct"; today, however, the name of Hell Pond is in common use. And so it is that Devil's Bridge, the adjacent Pluto's Grotto, and Hell Pond combine to form a netherworld of sorts or, as it is often called simply and pithily, a Hell. Although the area was laid out in this manner only after the time of Friedrich II (there had been basins and a small cascade here before)

---

7 Hirschfeld 1785, vol. 5, p. 236.

Ludwig Strack depicts a view over Hell Pond, with Devil's Bridge to the right, towards the Grand Fountain and the Palace far in the distance.

In the course of the ten-minute display, approximately 400 cubic metres of water tumble down the Devil's Bridge waterfall.

it still conforms to the Early Romantic/Sentimental gardening style in its intent to evoke feelings of eeriness and fright.

⑳ Pluto's Grotto

Pluto's Grotto was built in 1766–1768 on the site of the earlier Moritz Grotto (c. 1615); in a way, it represents the point of origin of the Weissenstein Park. It was designed to depict the realm of Pluto, god of the netherworld, and populated with statues of the mythological denizens of that realm: Proserpina, Pluto's spouse; Orpheus and Eurydice; Rhadamanthus, Furies, and others. The doorway was guarded by the hellhound Cerberus, whom only Hercules ever managed to overcome. The sculptures were mostly made of wood or plaster, and were lost around 1800 due to damp and vandalism. The only surviving speci-

Pluto's Grotto, framed by conifers and a dark copper beech

mens are two sandstone sculptures (currently in storage) by Johann August Nahl the Elder (1710–1781); they were positioned to flank the grotto, and depict fighting dragons and serpents. Originally they had been commissioned by Wilhelm VIII for the cascade in front of Wilhelmsthal Palace, but when Wilhelm IX decided to convert that park into another landscape garden, and the cascade was demolished, they were relocated to Pluto's Grotto in 1798.

To achieve an eerie, underworldly effect, the grotto's doors were fitted with panes of red-streaked glass. Now the doors have been reinstalled in the course of the State of Hesse's Projekt Museumslandschaft Kassel, the world turns red on entering the Grotto. Nahl's dragons, too, will be returning in due course to guard the entrance.

Detour: The Baroque axis

Pluto's Grotto and Hell Pond are situated on the park's central axis, and integrated into the original Baroque layout on several levels. For one, the netherworld they represent complements the pantheon of Classical mythology – the Olympian gods, the Titans and Neptune. For another, even Landgrave Carl's ideal design envisioned an elaborate structure in this very place. For those reasons, a brief detour to the park's Baroque beginnings would seem to be in order here.

The central axis is still in place and clearly visible even today; however, it is not, as Baroque axes usually are, a thoroughfare for the use of pedestrians or vehicles. The way up is via the park's main footpath to Neptune's Basin, and on by way of the Serpent Avenue laid out by Jussow to the foot of the Octagon. Alternatively and for those not averse to stairs, there is a shorter but more arduous route. It starts north of the Grotto, leading up the steps of the so-called Chicken Path, past Jussow's octagonal Felseneck Pavilion (1794), and on to Neptune's Basin. The original Felseneck, then called the Retraite, had three rooms – a vestibule, a cloakroom, and a closet or small study. In place of today's roof, it had a ruinous-looking parapet wall. It was

The path to Neptune's Basin takes visitors past the Felseneck Pavilion hidden in the forest. It offers the opportunity to rest after the stairs of the Chicken Path.

Wilhelm IX who commissioned the small, mock-ruinous but remarkably livable building. After 1872, the internal walls were removed, and the roof received its present-day shape.

From Neptune's Basin, the most direct route up is to take the stairs next to the Grand Cascade – another 535 or alternatively 539 steps will take the visitor to the top of Karlsberg hill. It is possible, however, to combine both routes: they both lead past Neptune's Plateau, where a view over the entire Baroque ensemble opens up.

Since the early 19th century there have always been restaurants in the park, both at the level of Neptune's Basin and north of the Octagon. Refreshments will be available after the climb!

The Octagon building with the copper statue of Hercules on the hilltop, and the water displays at its foot, constitute an ensemble that is unique in the world. The magnificent water axis was to become the core of the park. Although only about a third of the original plans, immortalised in the engravings by the Italian architect Giovanni Francesco Guerniero, was actually built by 1717, Landgrave Carl's vision has imprinted itself on the park and the city of Kassel to the present day.

Each of the later design phases made reference to it, carrying on the original idea in its own gardening style. The basic theme of the Baroque layout is the mythological Gigantomachy. The giants are enemies of the Olympian gods, and challenge them to a fierce battle. The Olympians carry the day because of the timely assistance of Hercules. Now the hero stands in a high place, looking out over the world spread out at his feet. A lone giant, Enceladus, almost crushed by a rock, spits a 12-m jet of water at the victorious hero with the last of his strength. (In the original, pre-1717 design he was to spit it at the Olympians.)

The statue of Hercules atop the Octagon marks the highest point of the Baroque ensemble, a structure apart yet intricately connected with, and integrated into, the landscape park. The spruce trees lining the Grand Cascade were planted for the purpose of partially obscuring the Octagon, arousing visitors' curiosity and tempting them to climb the hill.

Crushed by the weight of Mount Etna, the giant Enceladus spits a jet of water at his vanquishers – originally the Olympian gods, today, Hercules alone.

The copper-wrought statue was created in the years 1713–1717 by the Augsburg goldsmith Johann Jacob Anthoni (1674 or 1675–1725).

Above the Enceladus sculpture of the Giant's Head Basin is the Upper Water Theatre, which is also the first of the water displays: it features the Curved Cascades flanking the plateau, the fountains of the Artichoke Basin, and the Water-Trick Grotto at the back, which offers a very Baroque diversion. The floor is studded with small jets squirting water upwards. The contraption allows the unexpected soaking of visitors from below, and probably caused general merriment at the time. The grotto's dominant feature, though, is the statue of Pan playing his pipes, accompanied by the figures of Time (Chronos holding an hourglass and a scythe) and Envy (Invidia with a serpent). Originally the music for the panpipes was supplied by a water organ; this, however, has been in storage since the late 1960s at least.

The 8.30-m statue of Hercules, a replica of the Hercules Farnese, is a masterpiece in every respect. Its exposed location demanded a construction that had to be sturdy while being comparatively lightweight. A solid sculpture of either stone or bronze would not have served the

purpose. To make installing the statue on top of the 26-m Pyramid at all possible, an iron armature anchored in the Pyramid's masonry was developed, and the pre-fabricated parts of the statue were riveted on to it. The copper sheets were first beaten into shape in the Landgravial copper smithy of Bettenhausen (Kassel). The finely wrought repoussé was added in the workshop of Johann Jakob Anthoni, a goldsmith from Augsburg whom Carl had entrusted with this extraordinary task. The pieces were then soldered together into 21 precision-shaped, ready-to-assemble body parts, transported to the building site, mounted onto the armature, and riveted together. The approach is reminiscent of today's prefabricated construction methods, but it was completely unheard of at the time. Due to the "piecemeal" construction, it is still possible even today to remove individual parts for repair and put them back into place. The workmanship of the wrought copper has remained unsurpassed to the present day; even individual locks of hair are clearly visible from the platform of the Octagon, 40 m below. In keeping with the Absolutist self-image of the Baroque ruler, the Greek demigod Hercules was significant not only in the context of a Baroque layout but also as a reference to the ruling prince himself, Landgrave Carl.

The demonstration of power was a fundamental principle of the entire layout. In his carefully orchestrated water displays, Carl demonstrated his mastery of the forces of nature. The Artichoke Basin is a rather restrained example. By the time the water tumbles down into the Giant's Head Basin, possibly modelled on the waterfalls of Terni that Carl had visited during his tour of Italy, the displays have already grown considerably more impressive.

In this case Carl deliberately commissioned a natural-looking waterfall to contrast with the geometric regularity of the Semicircular Cascades

The Kassel Hercules, modelled on the statue of Hercules in the Roman Palazzo Farnese, was copper-wrought by Johann Jakob Anthoni, who completed it on 30 November, 1717. The statue is of outstanding workmanship. It depicts Hercules with his traditional attributes, the club and the skin of the Nemean Lion.

In his right hand, held behind his back, Hercules clasps the golden fruits of the Hesperides.

framing the basin, and the Grand Cascade at its foot. The latter again demonstrates both the elemental force of the water, and its taming by the hand of the Landgrave. The rushing of the water as it runs down the Cascades is inescapable; it surrounds and pursues visitors making their way down the hill. Occasionally it will escape its confines, and splashes of water hit the stairs (or the visitor). For all that it has been subjected to the will of Man, and runs downhill on a course prescribed for it.

㉑ Steinhöfer Waterfall

In the early 1790s the pipe-casting specialist Karl Steinhofer had been commissioned to complement the water supply by bringing in water from the Drusel stream in the adjacent Druseltal (Drusel valley). The water was conducted across the slope for more than 2 km, and then allowed to run downhill, for which purpose Steinhofer constructed a cascade of several small waterfalls.

It was considered so appropriate to the general scenery that it was subsequently enlarged, resulting in the Steinhöfer Waterfall and yet another major water feature. The waterfall was built to resemble a long-abandoned quarry reclaimed by Nature, in this case a forest. In

Like a relentless force of nature the water comes gushing on the entire width of the Steinhöfer Waterfall.

fact it was called the Forest Waterfall at first, a name very much in keeping with the era's romantic idealisation of Nature. With the building of the magnificent waterfall, Steinhofer finally emerged from the shadow of Jussow, with whom he had been working on a number of other projects, among them the Devil's Bridge waterfall, to become a notable water architect in his own right.

To allow for the display, the water must be dammed up first. Once the valves are opened, 430 cubic metres of water come gushing over the fall within ten minutes, and rush downhill over the craggy rocks, where it is collected again into a stream running on towards the Fountain Reservoir. Spreading relentlessly over the entire width of the steep slope, the water represents the primeval force of the untamed element. At the same time the hidden, yet nevertheless deliberate manipulation of the floods reminds spectators of the power of the Landgraves who harnessed the element.

22 Löwenburg (Lion Castle)

The artificial ruin of Löwenburg is another contribution by the architect Heinrich Christoph Jussow. It was built in the years 1793–1801 (the precincts were completed in 1803) in a neo-Gothic style.

An elaborate ensemble situated on a spur opposite the Palace, the Löwenburg with its tiltyard, castle and vegetable gardens, Wolves' Glen and vineyard stands out in every sense of the word.

It is both a fine structure in its own right, and a remarkable legacy of its era. The reference to the age of German chivalry expresses a longing for the virtues associated with that age, and at the same time the ruin, with its subtly implied status of an ancestral castle, stands for the long tradition of the ruling house of Hesse-Kassel.

Ludwig Strack depicts the castle at its most defiant, with the keep towering over the Woves' Glen.

View of Löwenburg and its chapel from the south-west – a romantic vision that is almost part of the natural landscape.

However, both the structure's well-fortified character and its ruinous state are purely cosmetic. From the beginning the castle was intended to be both residence and eventual burial place for its patron, Wilhelm IX. In WWII the Löwenburg suffered heavy damage, and restoration work has been going on for several years now. With the reconstruction of the war-destroyed keep, projected to start in 2014, the castle will regain its original appearance. Fortunately much of the furniture and fittings had been put into storage before the air raid, so that part of the original décor survives. A guided tour takes visitors through the suite of staterooms, arranged after the manner of a Baroque palace.

Additional highlights are the armoury, with many of the exhibits collected by Wilhelm IX himself, and the chapel built over the crypt of its patron.

㉓ Löwenburg precincts

The Löwenburg ensemble includes the tiltyard to the south, the vegetable garden and lawn in the west, the vineyard and Wolves' Glen

The armoury and the Black Knight

in the east, and the castle garden in the north. Schaeffer's plan of 1796 also shows a gigantic waterfall tumbling down into the so-called Wolves' Glen; the large Asch Reservoir was built specifically to provide the necessary water. When the vegetation in the Wolves' Glen was cleared in the course of a general overhaul of the castle precincts in 2011, the measures originally planned by Wilhelm IX, and the degree of completion they had reached, became evident.

There is much fine detail to draw the eye during a visit to Löwenburg.

Even the purpose of the breached moat and the stones in the eastern forecourt is obvious now: the waterfall was to suggest the destruction of the fortifications during the storming of the castle, and the moat's water tumbling downhill.

View up the Wolves' Glen. The large tower houses the staircase of the missing keep. The original design envisioned the water tumbling down these rocks into the narrow gorge.

View from the Bower Wing down into the castle garden with the Quatrefoil Fountain and statue of Venus

The project had to be abandoned as it, too, would have required water from the Drusel stream – which was already needed for the great water displays of Devil's Bridge, Aqueduct and Grand Fountain. Presumably the amount of water would not have been sufficient to operate yet another display, and thus all that is left of the project is plans (see the Schaeffer plan of 1796, p. 20) and paintings. The Asch Pond, however, was maintained both as a reservoir for the Romantic-era water displays and as a woodland lake.

The castle garden is orientated towards the Bower Wing, and designed to evoke the days when the ladies of the Age of Chivalry spent their hours of leisure sitting by the gently splashing fountain. The statue of Venus and Amor on the central axis is an allegory of love. The layout of the severely geometric hedges, too, harks back to the medieval garden, with the fruit trees on the enclosed patches of lawn intended to help ensure the castle's self-sufficiency. All of it added to the illusion of a building seemingly from the Middle Ages, in a time when Europe's princes could no longer be so sure of their God-given right to rule, and perhaps liked to recall an age when their position had been beyond doubt and challenge.

In the north-western corner of the castle garden, just above the vine-yard, is a small arbour of lime trees. It offers visitors a breathtaking view over Wilhelmshöhe Palace and the city of Kassel.

24 Village of Mulang

When Friedrich II commissioned the Chinese Village in 1782, he embarked on his last project, which was also designed to expand the park considerably towards the south. The village owed its existence both to the then-current fashion for everything Chinese, and to a new fashion in landscape gardening: the creation of entire settlements, or "ornamental farms", as part of a mock-natural countryside. The decision to give the houses, designed by the architect Simon Louis du Ry, a "Chinese" appearance may also have something to do with the fact that Chinese farming was considered very progressive at the time, and a successful and productive peasantry was prerequisite to a flourishing state.

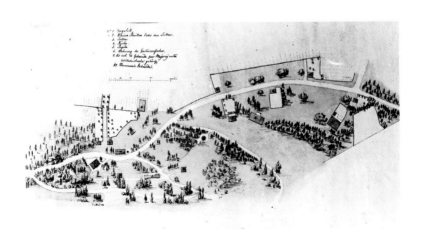

The plan, attributed to Wilhelm Hentze, depicts the village of Mulang around 1834, after the extensions by Wilhelm IX and the village's integration-by-landscaping into the park.

In order to prove that the village was real, farm work was actually carried out there: corn was ground at the mill, cattle were herded on the grassy slopes, and cheese and cream were produced in the Dairy. Success, however, was limited, as shown by the fact that only a few years later the buildings were let out on lease. By the 1830s, dairy processing took place at the old dairy farm once more.

After Friedrich's death his son, Wilhelm IX, extended the village towards the west, adding buildings such as the neo-Classical Spanish Sheepfold (today's Mulangstraße 8). Numerous structures have survived, among them the Pagoda (see below), the Kitchen, the Dairy, and residential buildings like the Bagatelle (Mulangstraße 2) and the former cowshed (Mulangstraße 5), the Custodian's House (Mulangstraße 3) and several shepherds' cottages (Mulangstraße 4, 6, and 9 as well as the front building of No. 10).

25 Chinese Pagoda

The Chinese Pagoda was built in 1777, an "atmospheric" building in the spirit of late Rococo and modelled on Charles Over's 1757 Banquetting House in London. Like the Mosque that once stood at the

The stone ogee arch of the Pagoda's doorway, guarded by a pair of dragons

The Pagoda, with the Palace in the background

village's entrance, it was intended to be a symbol of tolerance towards other religions. Above the door of the Pagoda, a pair of Chinese dragons guard the entrance; the columns are of coloured wood.

The interior once sheltered a statue of Confucius (of which only the torso remains), and a fake library made of wood gave the impression that Chinese books were kept here. A wind chime with an Oriental crescent moon tinkles in windy weather. A fine katsura tree (Cercidiphyllum), planted rather later, emphasises the exotic nature of the place. The Pagoda could be considered the cultural heart of the village. Its vivid colour, glazed roof tiles, and gilt decoration certainly draw the eye, although it is strictly speaking not even a pagoda, lacking as it does the towering roof structure with the multiple eaves.

26 Cemetery

The first burial on the new cemetery south of the park, at the junction of Schlossteichstraße and Mulangstraße, took place in 1817, although the cemetery was only consecrated in 1820. Soon the initial hedge was replaced by a wall; two stones on either side of the entrance bear inscriptions clarifying both the time and the purpose: "Wilhelminus I. 1820" and "Gottes Frieden über den Toten" ("God's Peace over the Dead").

At first, officials and servants entrusted with the shaping and maintenance of the park were buried here, and later persons of merit from the Wilhelmshöhe neighbourhood too. Among the notables laid to rest here are Inspector of Wells Karl Steinhofer; Chief Gardener Carl Sennholz; Garden Director Ernst Virchow and his wife Jenny; a senior and eminent civil servant, Hermann Schafft; and the founder of a Wilhelmshöher sanatorium, Moritz Wiederhold. At the Lac north of the cemetery our tour has come full circle. The lakeside path, or alternatively Mulangstraße, will take you to the central arrivals area, the Ochsenallee car park, the Wilhelmshöhe tram station inside the park, and the Visitor Centre Wilhelmshöhe.

The tramway terminal building by Georg Carl Wilhelm Kegel, built 1898. It was restored in 2008, and since then it has been in use as the Visitor Centre Wilhelmshöhe on the "city" side of the park. Another visitor centre has been built in the vicinity of the Hercules.

The tour will have taken you through three hundred years of the park's history, a history still immensely alive, relivable and explorable. Today the park is a place of culture and inspiration, a place for the enjoyment of art, and a place of recreation as it always has been.

"The Bergpark Wilhelmshöhe is of outstanding and universal value. Nowhere else in the world did man demonstrate his mastery over nature, represented by the element of water, by such a monumental display."[8]

---

8 Nomination for inscription of the park on the UNESCO World Heritage list.

Rear view of the Hercules statue atop the Pyramid

Timeline

1143 .... First mention of the Benedictine monastery Witzenstein.

1527............. Reformation and secularisation of Weissenstein Monastery by Philip I,
Landgrave of Hesse (1518–1567). Over time the monastery fell into
ruin but continued to be used for the hunt.

The Renaissance

1606............. The construction of a hunting lodge and summer residence with
landscape gardens and fishponds under Moritz, Landgrave of Hesse-
Kassel (1592–1627).

1615 / 1616..... The Moritz Grotto was constructed on the east slope of forest area
called Habichtswald (where the Pluto's Grotto now is). This sowed
the seeds for the Wilhelmshöhe water features and park. After the
Thirty Years' War the Moritz Grotto fell into decay.

Baroque Phase

1687............. Johann Hartmann Wessel was appointed court architect by Carl I,
Landgrave of Hesse-Kassel (1677–1730), and carried out the rock
detonations on the Winterkasten, the ridge on top of which the statue
of Hercules now stands.

From 1687 onwards ..... Construction on a cascade.

From 1796 onwards ..... On the Winterkasten extensive construction of sub-
terranean passageways and masonry work etc.

From 1698 onwards ..... Building Director Karl von Hattenbach managed
construction work on the Winterkasten.

From 1698 onwards ..... Sichelbach Reservoir was constructed to supply water for
the Baroque water features.

1699–1700 ... December to April: Carl I's trip to Italy where he visited numerous
gardens, villas, churches and sanatoria.

1701 .... Giovanni Francesco Guerniero signed his first contract with Carl I
for constructing water conduits for the Upper Water Theatre (Water-
Trick Grotto or Vexierwassergrotte) as well as for enhancing the
Octagon (ground storey).

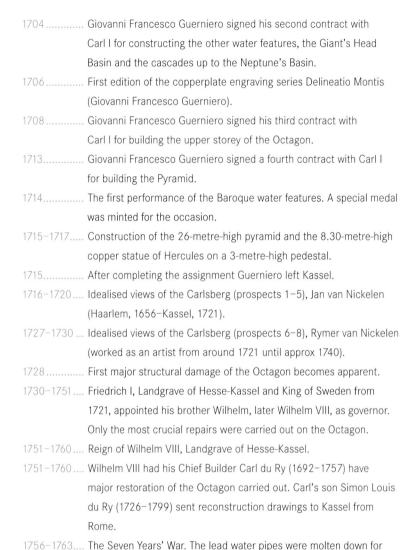

1704 .... Giovanni Francesco Guerniero signed his second contract with
Carl I for constructing the other water features, the Giant's Head
Basin and the cascades up to the Neptune's Basin.

1706 .... First edition of the copperplate engraving series Delineatio Montis
(Giovanni Francesco Guerniero).

1708 .... Giovanni Francesco Guerniero signed his third contract with
Carl I for building the upper storey of the Octagon.

1713 .... Giovanni Francesco Guerniero signed a fourth contract with Carl I
for building the Pyramid.

1714 .... The first performance of the Baroque water features. A special medal
was minted for the occasion.

1715–1717..... Construction of the 26-metre-high pyramid and the 8.30-metre-high
copper statue of Hercules on a 3-metre-high pedestal.

1715 .... After completing the assignment Guerniero left Kassel.

1716–1720 .... Idealised views of the Carlsberg (prospects 1–5), Jan van Nickelen
(Haarlem, 1656–Kassel, 1721).

1727–1730 ... Idealised views of the Carlsberg (prospects 6–8), Rymer van Nickelen
(worked as an artist from around 1721 until approx 1740).

1728 .... First major structural damage of the Octagon becomes apparent.

1730–1751 .... Friedrich I, Landgrave of Hesse-Kassel and King of Sweden from
1721, appointed his brother Wilhelm, later Wilhelm VIII, as governor.
Only the most crucial repairs were carried out on the Octagon.

1751–1760 .... Reign of Wilhelm VIII, Landgrave of Hesse-Kassel.

1751–1760 .... Wilhelm VIII had his Chief Builder Carl du Ry (1692–1757) have
major restoration of the Octagon carried out. Carl's son Simon Louis
du Ry (1726–1799) sent reconstruction drawings to Kassel from
Rome.

1756–1763 .... The Seven Years' War. The lead water pipes were molten down for
ammunition. In 1759 Wilhelm VIII fled Kassel for Rinteln.

Transition to an English Garden – early Romantic-sentimental phase

1760–1785 .... Reign of Friedrich II, Landgrave of Hesse-Kassel, who returned in
1763 from exile in Brunswick.

From 1763 onwards...... Extensions of Weissenstein Palace and the development of the gardens in its immediate vicinity. The central axis was laid out with a parterre (a formal level garden), new fountain and a fountain basin were built as well as an amphitheatre and a cabinet (or hedged enclosure), and the Pluto's Grotto was constructed (1766–1768).

From 1767 onwards...... Construction of Wilhelmshöher Allee (called Weissensteiner Allee until 1798).

From 1770 to the 1780s .... New segments were added on both sides of the central axis below the Neptune's Basin. They were designed in the early Romantic-sentimental landscape style. These sections included numerous small architectural structures and sculptures (the Pyramid; Virgil's Tomb; the Hermitages of Socrates, Plato, Democritus, and Heraclitus et al.; a rosarium; a total of over 50 attractions that address mythological, philosophical and Age-of-Enlightenment subject matter).

1777............. Construction of the Pagoda.

1779 .... Construction of the Mosque.

1780–1785 ... The Chinese park village of Mulang expanded the park to the south, with additional extensions following until 1791 by Wilhelm IX.

English Garden

1785–1821 ... Reign of Wilhelm IX, Landgrave of Hesse-Kassel, after 1803 Wilhelm I, Prince-Elector of Hesse.

From 1785 onwards ..... The areas of the park landscaped in the early Romantic-sentimental style were remodelled into a classical English landscape park. The architects and designers of the English landscape park are the building inspector (and later director) Heinrich Christoph Jussow (1754–1825), court gardener Daniel August Schwarzkopf (1758–1817) and fountain inspector Karl Steinhofer (1747–1829).

1785–1800 ... Most of the romantic water features were constructed.

1798 .... The park was renamed from Weissensteiner Park to Wilhelmshöhe; landscaping in the romantic style peaked at Wilhelmshöhe.

1793–1803 ... Construction of Löwenburg with surrounding gardens and features.

1803............. Hesse-Kassel was made an electorate.

1806–1813.... The French occupied the Lectorate of Hesse. The Prince-elector fled.

1807–13 .... Wilhelmshöhe Palace was renamed to Napoleonshöhe (Napoleon's summit) and was used by Jérôme, King of Westphalia, as his favourite seat.

1821–1847 ... Reign of Wilhelm II, Prince-elector of Hesse.

1822–1864 ... Wilhelm Hentze was made court-garden inspector (1793–1874) and was the royal garden director after 1854. From 1822 onwards: last extension of the park in the area of the New Waterfall and the construction of the Great Greenhouse.

1829 / 1830 ... Completion of the three-storey connection buildings of the palace.

1847–1866 ... Reign of Friedrich Wilhelm I, Elector of Hesse.

1864–1891 ... Court Gardener Franz Vetter (1824–1896). Clearing of the visual axes, first carpet bedding was added to the Bowlinggreen, many new plants and planting arrangements were added.

Prussian Province – the period of garden administration

1866–1918.... The Electorate of Hesse was annexed to Prussia. Kassel was made the capital of the Prussian province Hesse-Nassau. While Wilhelmshöhe was reserved for the use of the King of Prussia, the park was open to the public and under the management of the Preussische Krongutverwaltung (Prussian crown estate administration, with its headquarters in Potsdam-Sanssouci).

1867............. On 15 August Wilhelm I, King of Prussia, made Wilhelmshöhe Palace his summer residence. His sons Wilhelm and Henry attended Friedrichs-Gymnasium, a grammar school in Kassel. Excursions of the family to Wilhelmshöhe "with its gorgeous gardens".

From 1891 onwards...... Wilhelm II, German Emperor (r. 1888–1918), visited Wilhelmshöhe annually at the end of August. The area of the Flora's Vale to the Isle of Roses was reserved for his use as a private garden. Vetter was appointed garden director at Potsdam-Sanssouci.

1891–1898 ... Court Gardener Gustav Adolf Fintelmann (1846–1918) implemented Vetter's instructions and in 1898 was appointed his successor in Potsdam.

1898–1918.... Ernst Virchow (1858–1943) was the royal court gardener.

1903............. Ernst Virchow drafted the "Virchow Plan" as a consequence of hundreds of years of park development. The plan illustrates in differentiated way the park's structures, waterways, paths, lawns, meadows and wooded areas. The plan is still the basis for the design of the park today.

1918–1945.... The management of Wilhelmshöhe Palace and Park was taken over by the Verwaltung der Staatlichen Schlösser und Gärten Berlin (State palace and garden administration in Berlin). The Garden Director Dr. Rudolf Hörold (1882–1945/suicide) was responsible for the management of Wilhelmshöhe from 1918 until 1938, and was appointed to work for the garden management of Potsdam-Sanssouci in 1938.

1938–1959 ... Chief Garden Inspector Helmuth Junggebauer (d. 1959).

1943............. The last performance of the New Waterfall.

1943............. Major air raid on Wilhelmshöhe Palace on 22 October. The domes of the palace and the Temple of Mercury were destroyed.

From 1945 onwards ..... The palace building was renovated as well as the Hercules Monument, maintenance of the park as a *gesamtkunstwerk*.

1946............. The newly founded Vewaltung der Staatlichen Schlösser und Gärten Hessen (Hesse palaces and gardens administration) took over the management of Wilhelmshöhe.

From 1958 onwards ..... Helmuth Junggebauer was made park manager of Wilhelmshöhe and Karlsaue.

1959–1969 ... Garden Construction Inspector Alexander Bothman.

1963............. The Cascades and the romantic waterfalls were put back into operation, but the New Waterfall remained out of order.

1967............. The Octagon was reopened on 24 June.

1969–2003... Hermann Mielke BSc was park director.

2004–2005... Michael Boßdorf BSc was director of Außenstelle Kassel.

Museumslandschaft Hessen Kassel

From 2006 onwards..... Bergpark Wilhelmshöhe was made part of the Museumslandschaft Hessen Kassel, which was formed by the union of the Staatliche Museen Kassel and Außenstelle Kassel of the Verwaltung der Staatlichen Schlösser und Gärten Hessen. The three parks in Kassel of Wilhelmshöhe, Wilhelmsthal and Karlsaue were integrated into the Department of Gardens and Landscape Architecture (Hauptabteilung Gärten und Gartenarchitekturen) with a scientific management division. Since 2007 the manager of the department is the garden historian Siegried Hoß BSc.

From 2006 onwards..... The Museumslandschaft Kassel was restructured due to an investment programme of the State of Hesse (MLK-Project). The project includes major repairs and restoration of the water features, the Hercules Monument and the park conceits, the restoration of Löwenburg as well as the restoration and extension of outhouses on the palace terrace.

2006–2007... Park director Siegfried Hoß BSc.

2007 .... Publication of *Park Wilhelmshöhe Kassel: Parkpflegewerk*.

2007–2011 ... Under the title of "Water Features and Hercules Monument in Wilhelmshöhe Mountain Park", a group of scholars and experts from various disciplines and departments drafted the application for the park, the adjacent summit of the range and the surrounding catchment area to be added to the UNESCO World Heritage List.

2008 .... Acting director Kai Lipphardt.

From 2009 onwards... Director Lutz Leutner (degree in forestry).

2012 .... Application sent to UNESCO's World Heritage Office in Paris.

2013 .... The committee of the UN cultural body recognised the outstanding universal value of the Bergpark Wilhelmshöhe and added it to its list of World Heritage Sites at the meeting that took place in June 2013 in Phnom Penh.

Glossary

Bowlinggreen

In a landscape park, the bowling green (as in the case of the Pleasureground, the compound spelling is a specialty of German gardening) is a large, flat, carefully manicured lawn adjacent to the palace or stately home. The game of bowls or boule was popular in both England and France as early as the beginning of the 16th century, and the immaculate lawns it required became a feature of the Baroque garden. There the bowling green was usually situated in a bosquet – a severely laid out block of trees or small forest.

The landscape garden's bowling green shares with its predecessor the manicured surface of short grass. However, its function here is entirely different: it provides the open space necessary for a proper appreciation of the main building. Situated in front of the house or palace, the bowling green – occasionally called boulingrin – replaces the generous parterres of the Baroque layout. The Wilhelmshöhe Bowlinggreen, like that of most gardens, is part of the Pleasureground.

Clumps

Clumps are sizeable arrangements of trees and shrubs of different types, combined so as to form a harmonious whole. They are more dense and solid than groups; often shrubs are deliberately placed to fill in the outline, or the trees' branches reach to the ground. For that reason clumps effectively block the view when in leaf, and lend themselves to the creation of separate garden spaces.

Elysium

In Greek mythology, Elysium or the Elysian Fields is a name for the Isles of the Blessed situated by, or in, the stream of Okeanos.

Flower clumps

Flower clumps are made up of a mix of herbaceous perennials, occasionally combined with small shrubs and annuals. They are set into the lawn and designed to make up a harmonious whole. One characteristic is the use of plants of different height, not strictly graded, with the tallest deliberately planted off-centre to achieve an impression of natural growth.

Folly

Decorative park building, largely nonfunctional and often exotic or downright extravagant in appearance.

Ornamental farm

A functional agricultural estate in keeping with the aesthetic priorities of the landscape garden. At Kassel this was extended into an entire settlement, the "Chinese Village", containing both functional buildings and elaborate follies.

Park buildings

Park buildings (often called "Staffagen" in German) are small structures for the embellishment of parks. They may be dedicated to a theme or person, e.g. a mythological concept or a philosopher. Sometimes also called follies, although follies tend to be more elaborate and/or extravagant.

Pleasureground

In landscape parks, the pleasure ground is an area of garden adjacent to the main house or palace. It replaced the traditional parterres of the Baroque garden, such as the orangery parterre or parterre de broderie, with their elaborate beds. Pleasure grounds feature manicured lawns and a more elaborate and openly decorative planting scheme than the rest of the garden.

Service buildings ("Ökonomie")

All the facilities needed for the running and supplying of a large estate such as a palace, including the main kitchens, the stables, carriage house and so on.

Styx

In Greek mythology, Styx is one of the rivers that form the boundary between the world of the living and the netherworld (Hades). The ferryman Charon transported the dead across the river; a coin placed in the mouth or on the eye of the deceased was to serve as the ferryman's fee.

View over Bergpark Wilhelmshöhe

Bibliography

Unprinted sources

Nominierungsdossier Wasserkünste und Herkules im Bergpark Wilhelmshöhe –
Nominierung zur Eintragung in die UNESCO Welterbeliste, 9-2011, Deutschland,
Hessisches Ministerium für Wissenschaft und Kunst
http://www.alt-zweibruecken.de/persoenlichkeiten/buerger/carlsteinhoffer,
Stand: 6. Juni 2013

References

David August von Apell: Cassel und die umliegende Gegend. Eine Skizze für
Reisende, Kassel, 1792

Horst Becker und Christiane Homburg: Schlosspark Wilhelmshöhe Kassel – Größter
Bergpark Europas – Landschaftspark mit Herkules und barocker Kaskadenanlage,
Broschüre 14 Edition der Verwaltung der Staatlichen Schlösser und Gärten Hessen,
Regensburg 2002

Horst Becker und Michael Karkosch: Park Wilhelmshöhe Kassel, Parkpflegewerk,
Monographien Band 8 Edition der Verwaltung der Staatlichen Schlösser und Gärten
Hessen, Regensburg 2007

William Chambers: Plans, Elevations, Sections and Perspective Views of the Gardens and Buildings at Kew in Surrey, London 1763, Reprint Farnborough 1966

Hans-Christoph Dittscheid: Kassel Wilhelmshöhe und die Krise des Schloßbaues am
Ende des Ancien Regime, Diss., Worms 1987

Wilhelm Döring: Kurze Beschreibung von Wilhelmshöhe bey Cassel, Kassel 1799

Karl Goetze: Album der Teppichgärtnerei und Gruppenpflanzungen, 3. Auflage, neu
bearbeitet durch Paul Böhme zu Wilhelmshöhe bei Kassel und Robert Engelhardt in
Erfurt, Ludwig Möller, Erfurt o. J. [1900]

Claudia Gröschel: Der Steinhöfer Wasserfall im Bergpark Wilhelmshöhe, in: Denkmalpflege in Hessen, hrsg. vom Landesamt für Denkmalpflege Hessen, Heft
2/1993, p. 34-35

Claudia Gröschel: Das Große Pflanzenhaus in der Wilhelmshöhe, in: Denkmalpflege
in Hessen, hrsg. vom Landesamt für Denkmalpflege Hessen, Heft 2/1993, p. 52-33

Claudia Gröschel: Wilhelm Hentze - ein Gartenkünstler des 19. Jahrhunderts, Diss.,
Universität Bern 1996

Giovanni Francesco Guerniero: Delineatio montis a metropoli Hasso-Casselana (...),
hrsg. von Harri Günther, Nachwort von Helmut Scharf, Stuttgart und Leipzig 1988
(Nachdruck der Ausgabe Kassel) 1706/1717

Justinian Freiherr von Günderode: Briefe eines Reisenden über den gegenwärtigen
Zustand von Cassel mit aller Freiheit geschildert, Frankfurt/M. und Leipzig 1781

Michael Hannwacker: Carlsberg bei Kassel. Der Weißenstein unter Landgraf Carl,
Diss. GHK Kassel, Kassel 1992

Paul Heidelbach: Geschichte der Wilhelmshöhe, Leipzig 1909

Dieter Hennebo und Alfred Hoffmann: Geschichte der deutschen Gartenkunst,
3 Bde., Hamburg 1962–65

Christian Cay Lorenz Hirschfeld: Theorie der Gartenkunst, 5 Bde., M. G. Weidmanns
Erben und Reich, Leipzig 1779-1785

Alfred Hoffmann: Park Wilhelmshöhe. Amtlicher Führer der Verwaltung der Staatlichen Schlösser und Gärten Hessen, Bad Homburg v. d. H., (um 1975)

Alois Holtmeyer: Die Bau- und Kunstdenkmäler im Regierungsbezirk Cassel, Bd. 4,
Marburg 1919

Alois Holtmeyer (Hrsg.): W. Strieder's Wilhelmshöhe, in: Alt Hessen. Beiträge zur
kunstgeschichtlichen Heimatkunde, Heft 3. Marburg 1913

Siegfried Hoss: Der Habichtswald – Quelle der Wasserkunst des Schlossparks
Wilhelmshöhe, in: Thilo F. Warneke: Lebensraum Habichtswald, Kassel 2010,
p. 104–117

Johann Christian Krieger: Cassel in historischtopographischer Hinsicht. Nebst einer
Geschichte und Beschreibung von Wilhelmshöhe und seinen Anlagen, Marburg
1805

Landesamt für Denkmalpflege (Hrsg.): Hortus ex Machina. Der Bergpark Wilhelmshöhe im Dreiklang von Kunst, Natur und Technik, Arbeitshefte des Landesamtes für
Denkmalpflege, Bd. 16, Stuttgart 2010

G. A. Lobe: Wanderungen durch Cassel und die Umgegend – Eine Skizze für Einhe-
imische und Fremde, Kassel 1887

Kai Mathieu (Hrsg.): Rosensammlung zu Wilhelmshöhe: Nach der Natur gemalt von
Salomon Pinhas, Kurfürstlicher Hof-Miniaturmaler 1815, Regensburg 2001

Matthäus Merian: Topographia Hassiae (...), Frankfurt/M. 1655

Bernd Modrow: Gartendenkmalpflege am Beispiel des Parkes Wilhelmshöhe, in:
Denkmalpflege in Hessen, hrsg. vom Landesamt für Denkmalpflege Hessen, Heft
2/1995, p. 16-24

Bernd Modrow und Monika Vogt: O, wonnevolle Gärten, hrsg. von der Sparkassen-
Kulturstiftung Hessen-Thüringen und dem Landesamt für Denkmalpflege Hessen,
Frankfurt/M. 2000

Conrad Mönch: Verzeichniß ausländischer Bäume und Stauden des Lustschlosses
Weißenstein bei Cassel, Frankfurt/M. und Leipzig 1785

Hans Ottomeyer und Christiane Lukatis (Hrsg. Staatliche Museen Kassel): Heinrich-
Christoph Jussow. 1754–1825. Ein hessischer Architekt des Klassizismus, Worms
1999

Charles Over: Ornamented Architecture in the Gothic, Chinese and Modern Taste,
London 1758

Karl Paetow: Klassizismus und Romantik auf Wilhelmshöhe, Kassel 1929

Antje Scherner: Giovanni Francesco Guerniero – Ein Architekt aus dem Umkreis
Carlo Fontanas? Neue Quellen zu Leben und Werk des Baumeisters der Kasseler
Wasserspiele – Sonderdruck, aus: Marburger Jahrbuch für Kunstwissenschaften,
Bd. 38, Weimar 2001

Ulrich Schmidt: Der Schloßpark Wilhelmshöhe in Ansichten der Romantik, hrsg. von
Staatliche Museen Kassel und Verwaltung der Staatlichen Schlösser und Gärten
Hessen, Kassel 1993

Friedrich Christoph Schmincke: Versuch einer genauen und umständlichen
Beschreibung der hochfürstlich-hessischen Residenz- und Hauptstadt Cassel nebst
den nahe gelegenen Lustschlössern, Gärten und andern sehenswürdigen Sachen,
Kassel 1767

Johann Friedrich Armand Uffenbach: Tagebuch einer Spazierfahrth durch die hessi-
chen in die braunschweig-lüneburgische Lande, 1728, veröffentlicht von Max Arnim,
Göttingen 1928

Heike Zech: Kaskaden in der deutschen Gartenkunst des 18. Jahrhunderts. Vom
architektonischen Brunnen zum naturimitierenden Wasserfall, Wien 2010

List of illustrations

p. 8: Ernst Happel, Kloster Weißenstein, um 1550, Reproduktion aus: Paul Heidelbach: Geschichte der Wilhelmshöhe, Klinkhardt & Biermann, Leipzig 1909, p. 1

p. 9: Kassel, Wilhelmshöhe von der Allee aus, aus: Album »Cassel und Wilhelmshöhe«, 1880, Hessisches Staatsarchiv Darmstadt, R 4 Nr. 20967/4A

p. 10: Alessandro Specchi nach Giovanni Francesco Guerniero, Ansicht des Palastes am Fuße des Berges, in: Delineatio Montis, 1706, MHK, Graphische Sammlung, GS 27989

p. 12: Girolamo Frezza nach Giovanni Francesco Guerniero, Ansicht des Oktogons und der Grottenanlagen am Vexierwasserplateau, in: Delineatio Montis, 1705, MHK, Graphische Sammlung, GS 12478

p. 13: Wolfgang Mayr nach Johann Georg Fünck, Prospekt des Karlsberges, 1760, MHK, Graphische Sammlung, GS 9746

p. 15: Carl Ferdinand Bosse, Plan des Hochfürstl. Landgraeflichen Hessischen Lustschlosses und neu angelegten Gartens zum Weissenstein, nebst dass dabey liegende berühmte Gebäude, und köstliche Wasserwerck des Carlsberges. aufgenommen und gezeichnet von Carl Ferdinand Bosse Ao. 1776, 1776, Architekturmuseum TU Berlin, Inv. Nr. 11668

p. 16: Johann Heinrich Tischbein d. Ä.: Schloss und Park Weißenstein von Südwesten, Situation um 1766, Hessische Hausstiftung, Schloss Fasanerie, FAS B 341

p. 18: Andreas Range nach unbekannt, Prospekt des Fürstlichen Schlosses auf dem Weißenstein von der Abendseite, 1791, MHK, Graphische Sammlung, GS 27326

p. 20: Caspar Christoph Schaeffers, Plan des Weissenstein mit allen daselbst befindlichen Anlagen und Gebäuden, 1796, MHK, Schlossmuseen, SM 1.3.815

p. 22: Johann Heinrich Müntz, Aushub des Lac, 1786, aus: Desseins de Müntz de Wilhelmshoehe, 27 Tafeln, 1789–1796, VSG 6.2.389, fol. 9 (11)

p. 23: Johann Heinrich B. Bleuler (1787–1857), Der Steinhöffersche Wasserfall gegen die Löwenburg, 1826, MHK, Graphische Sammlung, GS 12654

p. 26: Johann Heinrich B. Bleuler (1787–1857), Das Churfürstliche Lust-Schloss Wilhelmshöhe, 1825, MHK, Graphische Sammlung, GS 20366

p. 27: Heinrich Martens, nach Conrad Löwer, Darstellung des mit Wasser überströmten Neuen Wasserfalls, um 1835/40, Stadtmuseum Kassel, Sammlung Lometsch, SLo 137

p. 29: Matthias Bernhard und Johann Conrad Beck (?), Teekanne mit einer Ansicht des Gewächshauses, um 1825, MHK, Sammlung Angewandte Kunst, Reproduktion aus: Ulrich Schmidt (Hrsg.): Der Schloßpark Wilhelmshöhe in Ansichten der Romantik, Bad Homburg vor der Höhe, 1993, p. 71

p. 31: Ernst Virchow, Plan vom Park Wilhelmshöhe, 1903, MHK, Schlossmuseen, SM 1.3.1117

p. 38: Salomon Pinhas (1759–1837), Rose. Perle. De Weisssenstein, aus: Rosenalbum: Rosen-Sammlung zu Wilhelmshoehe, 148 Blätter, Tafel 63, 1815, MHK, Graphische Sammlung, SM-GS 6.2.391

p. 38: Johann Heinrich Tischbeins d. Ä., Ansicht des Schlosses Weißenstein von Westen, 1786/1787, MHK, Schlossmuseen, SM 1.1.102, Detail

p. 41: Johann Heinrich Tischbein d. Ä. (1722–1789), Ansicht des Schlosses Weißenstein von Süden, 1786, MHK, Schlossmuseen, SM 1.1.524

p. 57: Johann Gottlieb Kobold (1769–1809), Höhle der Sibille, 1795, MHK, Graphische Sammlung, GS 21651

p. 60: Ludwig Philipp Strack (1761–1836), Blick vom Bergpark auf Schloß Wilhelmshöhe von Westen, um 1800, MHK, Graphische Sammlung, GS 20264

p. 70: Ludwig Philipp Strack (1761–1836), Löwenburg von unten, vor 1798, MHK, Schlossmuseen, SM 1.1.1014

p. 75: Wilhelm Hentze (Umkreis?), Plan von Moulang, nach 1834, StAM, VSG Neg-Nr. 5744, Fotoreproduktion, Bad Homburg v. d. H.

Picture credits

Architekturmuseum TU Berlin: p. 15

Hessische Hausstiftung, Schloss Fasanerie: p. 16 (unten)

Hessisches Staatsarchiv Darmstadt: p. 9

Siegfried Hoß: p. 53, 79

MHK: p. 8, 10, 12, 13, 16 (oben), 18, 20, 21, 23, 26, 28 (unten), 29, 38 (unten), 39, 41, 42, 44, 46, 47, 54, 55, 56, 57, 59, 60 (oben), 62, 64, 66, 69

MHK (Ute Brunzel): p. 22, 70

MHK (Gerald Geyer): Titel, p. 6, 34/35, 36, 40, 43, 45, 48, 50, 51, 52, 60 (unten), 63, 65, 68, 71, 72, 73, 74, 76, 77, 80, 89

MHK (Roman Götz): p. 28 (oben)

MHK (Frank Mihm): p. 31, 38 (oben)

Stadtmuseum Kassel: p. 27

Typoscape (Rolf Eusterschulte): Bergparkplan, hintere Umschlagklappe

VSG: p. 75

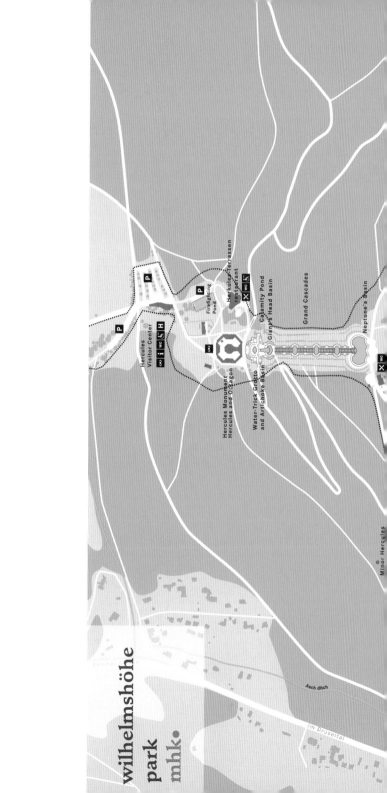

wilhelmshöhe
park
mhk•

Hercules
Visitor Center

Firefighting
Pond

Herkules-Terrassen
Restaurant

Hercules Monument
Hercules and Octagon

Water-Trick Grotto
and Artichoke Basin

Calamity Pond

Giant's Head Basin

Grand Cascades

Neptune's Basin

Minor Hercules

Asch ditch

im Druseltal